What is Coming?

A Forecast of Things after the War

H. G. WELLS

1st WORLD
LIBRARY
Literary Society

What is Coming?

H. G. Wells

© 1st World Library, 2007
PO Box 2211
Fairfield, IA 52556
www.1stworldlibrary.com
First Edition

LCCN: 2007920654

Softcover ISBN: 978-1-4218-3962-2
Hardcover ISBN: 978-1-4218-3862-5
eBook ISBN: 978-1-4218-4062-8

Purchase *"What is Coming?"*
as a traditional bound book at:
www.1stWorldLibrary.com/purchase.asp?ISBN=978-1-4218-3962-2

1st World Library is a literary, educational organization
dedicated to:

- Creating a free internet library of downloadable ebooks

- Hosting writing competitions and offering book
  publishing scholarships.

1ˢᵗ World Library Literary Society

Giving Back to the World

"If you want to work on the core problem, it's early school literacy."
- **James Barksdale, former CEO of Netscape**

"No skill is more crucial to the future of a child, or to a democratic and prosperous society, than literacy."

- **Los Angeles Times**

Literacy... means far more than learning how to read and write... The aim is to transmit... knowledge and promote social participation."
- **UNESCO**

"Literacy is not a luxury, it is a right and a responsibility. If our world is to meet the challenges of the twenty-first century we must harness the energy and creativity of all our citizens."

- **President Bill Clinton**

"Parents should be encouraged to read to their children, and teachers should be equipped with all available techniques for teaching literacy, so the varying needs and capacities of individual kids can be taken into account."
- **Hugh Mackay**

CONTENTS

I

FORECASTING THE FUTURE

Prophecy may vary between being an intellectual amusement and a serious occupation; serious not only in its intentions, but in its consequences. For it is the lot of prophets who frighten or disappoint to be stoned. But for some of us moderns, who have been touched with the spirit of science, prophesying is almost a habit of mind.

Science is very largely analysis aimed at forecasting. The test of any scientific law is our verification of its anticipations. The scientific training develops the idea that whatever is going to happen is really here now—if only one could see it. And when one is taken by surprise the tendency is not to say with the untrained man, "Now, who'd ha' thought it?" but "Now, what was it we overlooked?"

Everything that has ever existed or that will ever exist is here—for anyone who has eyes to see. But some of it demands eyes of superhuman penetration. Some of it is patent; we are almost as certain of next Christmas and the tides of the year 1960 and the death before 3000 A.D. of everybody now alive as if these things had already happened. Below that level of certainty, but still at a very high level of certainty, there are such things as that men will probably be making aeroplanes of an improved pattern in 1950, or that there will be a through railway connection between Constantinople and Bombay and between Baku and Bombay in the next half-century. From such grades of certainty as this, one may come down the scale until the most obscure mystery of all is reached: the mystery of the individual. Will England presently produce a military genius? or what will Mr. Belloc say the day after to-morrow? The most accessible field for the prophet is the heavens; the least is the secret of the jumping cat within the human skull. How will so-and-so behave, and how will the nation take it? For such questions as that we need the subtlest guesses of all.

Yet, even to such questions as these the sharp, observant man may risk an answer with something rather better than an even chance of being right.

The present writer is a prophet by use and wont. He is more interested in to-morrow than he is in to-day, and the past is just material for future guessing. "Think of the men who have walked here!" said a tourist in the Roman Coliseum. It was a Futurist mind that answered: "Think of the men who will." It is surely as interesting that presently some founder of the World Republic, some obstinate opponent of militarism or legalism, or the man who will first release atomic energy for human use, will walk along the Via Sacra as that Cicero or Giordano Bruno or Shelley have walked there in the past. To the prophetic mind all history is and will continue to be a prelude. The prophetic type will steadfastly refuse to see the world as a museum; it will insist that here is a stage set for a drama that perpetually begins.

Now this forecasting disposition has led the writer not only to publish a book of deliberate prophesying, called "Anticipations," but almost without premeditation to scatter a number of more or less obvious prophecies through his other books. From first to last he has been writing for twenty years, so that it is possible to check a certain proportion of these antici-pations by the things that have happened, Some of these shots have hit remarkably close to the bull's-eye of reality; there are a number of inners and outers, and some clean misses. Much that he wrote about in anticipation is now established commonplace. In 1894 there were still plenty of sceptics of the possibility either of automobiles or aeroplanes; it was not until 1898 that Mr. S.P. Langley (of the Smithsonian Institute) could send the writer a photograph of a heavier-than-air flying machine actually in the air. There were articles in the monthly magazines of those days *proving* that flying was impossible.

One of the writer's luckiest shots was a description (in "Anticipations" in 1900) of trench warfare, and of a deadlock almost exactly upon the lines of the situation after the battle of the Marne. And he was fortunate (in the same work) in his estimate of the limitations of submarines. He anticipated Sir Percy Scott by a year in his doubts of the decisive value of great battleships (*see* "An Englishman Looks at the World"); and he was sound in denying the decadence of France; in doubting (before the Russo-Japanese struggle) the greatness of the power of Russia, which was still in those days a British bogey; in making Belgium the battle-ground in a coming struggle between the mid-European Powers and the rest of Europe; and (he believes) in foretelling a renascent Poland. Long before Europe was familiar with the engaging personality of the German Crown Prince, he represented great airships sailing over England (which country had been too unenterprising to make any) under the command of a singularly anticipatory Prince Karl, and in "The World Set Free" the last disturber of the peace is a certain "Balkan Fox."

In saying, however, here and there that "before such a year so-and-so will happen," or that "so-and-so will not occur for the next twenty years," he was generally pretty widely wrong; most of his time estimates are too short; he foretold, for example, a special motor track apart from the high road between London and Brighton before 1910, which is still a dream, but he doubted if effective military aviation or aerial fighting would be possible before 1950, which is a miss on the other side. He will draw a modest veil over certain still wider misses that the idle may find for themselves in his books; he prefers to count the hits and leave the reckoning of the misses to those who will find a pleasure in it.

Of course, these prophecies of the writer's were made upon a basis of very generalised knowledge. What can be done by a really sustained research into a particular question—especially if it is a question essentially mechanical—is shown by the work of a Frenchman all too neglected by the trumpet of fame— Clement Ader. M. Ader was probably the first man to get a mechanism up into the air for something more than a leap. His *Eole*, as General Mensier testifies, prolonged a jump as far as fifty metres as early as 1890. In 1897 his *Avion* fairly flew. (This is a year ahead of the date of my earliest photograph of S.P. Langley's aeropile in mid-air.) This, however, is beside our present mark. The fact of interest here is that in 1908, when flying was still almost incredible, M. Ader published his "Aviation Militaire." Well, that was eight years ago, and men have been fighting in the air now for a year, and there is still nothing being done that M. Ader did not see, and which we, if we had had the wisdom to attend to him, might not have been prepared for. There is much that he foretells which is still awaiting its inevitable fulfilment. So clearly can men of adequate knowledge and sound reasoning power see into the years ahead in all such matters of material development.

But it is not with the development of mechanical inventions that the writer now proposes to treat. In this book he intends to hazard certain forecasts about the trend of events in the next decade or so. Mechanical novelties will probably play a very small part in that coming history. This world-wide war means a general arrest of invention and enterprise, except in the direction of the war business. Ability is concentrated upon that; the types of ability that are not applicable to warfare are neglected; there is a vast destruction of capital and a waste of the savings that are needed to finance new experiments. Moreover, we are killing off many of our brightest young men.

It is fairly safe to assume that there will be very little new furniture on the stage of the world for some considerable time; that if there is much difference in the roads and railways and shipping it will be for the worse; that architecture, domestic equipment, and so on, will be fortunate if in 1924 they stand

H. G. Wells

where they did in the spring of 1914. In the trenches of France and Flanders, and on the battlefields of Russia, the Germans have been spending and making the world spend the comfort, the luxury and the progress of the next quarter-century. There is no accounting for tastes. But the result is that, while it was possible for the writer in 1900 to write "Anticipations of the Reaction of Mechanical Progress upon Human Life and Thought," in 1916 his anticipations must belong to quite another system of consequences.

The broad material facts before us are plain enough. It is the mental facts that have to be unravelled. It isn't now a question of "What thing—what faculty—what added power will come to hand, and how will it affect our ways of living?" It is a question of "How are people going to take these obvious things—waste of the world's resources, arrest of material progress, the killing of a large moiety of the males in nearly every European country, and universal loss and unhappiness?" We are going to deal with realities here, at once more intimate and less accessible than the effects of mechanism.

As a preliminary reconnaissance, as it were, over the region of problems we have to attack, let us consider the difficulties of a single question, which is also a vital and central question in this forecast. We shall not attempt a full answer here, because too many of the factors must remain unexamined; later, perhaps, we may be in a better position to do so. This question is the probability of the establishment of a long world peace.

At the outset of the war there was a very widely felt hope among the intellectuals of the world that this war might clear up most of the outstanding international problems, and prove the last war. The writer, looking across the gulf of experience that separates us from 1914, recalls two pamphlets whose very titles are eloquent of this feeling—"The War that will End War," and "The Peace of the World." Was the hope expressed in those phrases a dream? Is it already proven a dream? Or can we read between the lines of the war news, diplomatic disputations, threats and accusations, political wranglings and stories of hardship and cruelty that now fill our papers, anything that still justifies a hope that these bitter years of world sorrow are the darkness before the dawn of a better day for mankind? Let us handle this problem for a preliminary examination.

What is really being examined here is the power of human reason to prevail over passion—and certain other restraining and qualifying forces. There can be little doubt that, if one could canvass all mankind and ask them whether they would rather have no war any more, the overwhelming mass of them would elect for universal peace. If it were war of the modern mechanical type that was in question, with air raids, high explosives, poison gas and submarines, there could be no doubt at all about the response. "Give peace in our time, O Lord," is more than ever the common prayer of Christendom, and the very war makers claim to be peace makers; the German Emperor has never faltered in his assertion that he encouraged Austria to send an impossible ultimatum to Serbia, and invaded Belgium because Germany was being attacked. The Krupp-Kaiser Empire, he assures us, is no eagle, but a double-headed lamb, resisting the shearers and butchers. The apologists for war are in a hopeless minority; a certain number of German Prussians who think war good for the soul, and the dear ladies of the London *Morning Post* who think war so good for the manners of the working classes, are rare, discordant voices in the general chorus against war. If a mere unsupported and uncoordinated will for peace could realise itself, there would be peace, and an enduring peace, to-morrow. But, as a matter of fact, there is no peace coming to-morrow, and no clear prospect yet of an enduring universal peace at the end of this war.

Now what are the obstructions, and what are the antagonisms to the exploitation of this world-wide disgust with war and the world-wide desire for peace, so as to establish a world peace?

Let us take them in order, and it will speedily become apparent that we are dealing here with a subtle quantitative problem in

H. G. Wells

psychology, a constant weighing of whether this force or that force is the stronger. We are dealing with influences so subtle that the accidents of some striking dramatic occurrence, for example, may turn them this way or that. We are dealing with the human will—and thereby comes a snare for the feet of the would-be impartial prophet. To foretell the future is to modify the future. It is hard for any prophet not to break into exhortation after the fashion of the prophets of Israel.

The first difficulty in the way of establishing a world peace is that it is nobody's business in particular. Nearly all of us want a world peace—in an amateurish sort of way. But there is no specific person or persons to whom one can look for the initiatives. The world is a supersaturated solution of the will-for-peace, and there is nothing for it to crystallise upon. There is no one in all the world who is responsible for the understanding and overcoming of the difficulties involved. There are many more people, and there is much more intelligence concentrated upon the manufacture of cigarettes or hairpins than upon the establishment of a permanent world peace. There are a few special secretaries employed by philanthropic Americans, and that is about all. There has been no provision made even for the emoluments of these gentlemen when universal peace is attained; presumably they would lose their jobs.

Nearly everybody wants peace; nearly everybody would be glad to wave a white flag with a dove on it now—provided no unfair use was made of such a demonstration by the enemy—but there is practically nobody thinking out the arrangements needed, and nobody making nearly as much propaganda for the instruction of the world in the things needful as is made in selling any popular make of automobile. We have all our particular businesses to attend to. And things are not got by just wanting them; things are got by getting them, and rejecting whatever precludes our getting them.

That is the first great difficulty: the formal Peace Movement is quite amateurish.

It is so amateurish that the bulk of people do not even realise the very first implication of the peace of the world. It has not succeeded in bringing this home to them.

If there is to be a permanent peace of the world, it is clear that there must be some permanent means of settling disputes between Powers and nations that would otherwise be at war. That means that there must be some head power, some point of reference, a supreme court of some kind, a universally recognised executive over and above the separate Governments of the world that exist to-day. That does not mean that those Governments Have to disappear, that "nationality" has to be given up, or anything so drastic as that. But it does mean that all those Governments have to surrender almost as much of their sovereignty as the constituent sovereign States which make up the United States of America have surrendered to the Federal Government; if their unification is to be anything more than a formality, they will have to delegate a control of their inter-State relations to an extent for which few minds are prepared at present.

It is really quite idle to dream of a warless world in which States are still absolutely free to annoy one another with tariffs, with the blocking and squeezing of trade routes, with the ill-treatment of immigrants and travelling strangers, and between which there is no means of settling boundary disputes. More-over, as between the united States of the world and the United States of America there is this further complication of the world position: that almost all the great States of Europe are in possession, firstly, of highly developed territories of alien language and race, such as Egypt; and, secondly, of barbaric and less-developed territories, such as Nigeria or Madagascar. There will be nothing stable about a world settlement that does not destroy in these "possessions" the national preference of the countries that own them and that does not prepare for the immediate or eventual accession of these subject peoples to State rank. Most certainly, however, thousands of intelligent people in those great European countries who believe them-selves ardent for a world peace will be staggered at any proposal to place any part of "our Empire" under a world administration on the footing of a United States territory. Until they cease to be staggered by anything of the sort, their aspirations for a permanent peace will remain disconnected from the main current of their lives. And that current will flow, sluggishly or rapidly, towards war. For essentially these "possessions" are like tariffs, like the strategic occupation of neutral countries or secret treaties; they are forms of the conflict between nations to oust and prevail over other nations.

Going on with such things and yet deprecating war is really not an attempt to abolish conflict; it is an attempt to retain conflict and limit its intensity; it is like trying to play hockey on the understanding that the ball shall never travel faster than eight miles an hour.

Now it not only stands in our way to a permanent peace of the world that the great mass of men are not prepared for even the most obvious implications of such an idea, but there is also a second invincible difficulty—that there is nowhere in the world anybody, any type of men, any organisation, any idea, any nucleus or germ, that could possibly develop into the necessary over-Government. We are asking for something out of the air, out of nothingness, that will necessarily array against itself the resistance of all those who are in control, or interested in the control, of the affairs of sovereign States of the world as they are at present; the resistance of a gigantic network of Government organisations, interests, privileges, assumptions.

Against this a headless, vague aspiration, however universal, is likely to prove quite ineffective. Of course, it is possible to suggest that the Hague Tribunal is conceivably the germ of such an overriding direction and supreme court as the peace of the world demands, but in reality the Hague Tribunal is a mere legal automatic machine. It does nothing unless you set it in motion. It has no initiative. It does not even protest against the most obvious outrages upon that phantom of a world-conscience—international law.

Pacificists in their search for some definite starting-point, about which the immense predisposition for peace may crystallise, have suggested the Pope and various religious organisations as a possible basis for the organisation of peace. But there would be no appeal from such a beginning to the non-Christian majority of mankind, and the suggestion in itself indicates a profound ignorance of the nature of the Christian churches. With the exception of the Quakers and a few Russian sects, no Christian sect or church has ever repudiated war; most have gone out of the way to sanction it and bless it.

It is altogether too rashly assumed by people whose sentimentality outruns their knowledge that Christianity is essentially an attempt to carry out the personal teachings of Christ. It is nothing of the sort, and no church authority will support that idea. Christianity—more particularly after the ascendancy of the Trinitarian doctrine was established—was and is a theological religion; it is the religion that triumphed over Arianism, Manichseism, Gnosticism, and the like; it is based not on Christ, but on its creeds. Christ, indeed, is not even its symbol; on the contrary, the chosen symbol of Christianity is the cross to which Christ was nailed and on which He died. It was very largely a religion of the legions. It was the warrior Theodosius who, more than any single other man, imposed it upon Europe.

There is no reason, therefore, either in precedent or profession, for expecting any plain lead from the churches in this tremendous task of organising and making effective the widespread desire of the world for peace. And even were this the case, it is doubtful if we should find in the divines and dignitaries of the Vatican, of the Russian and British official churches, or of any other of the multitudinous Christian sects, the power and energy, the knowledge and ability, or even the goodwill needed to negotiate so vast a thing as the creation of a world authority.

One other possible starting-point has been suggested. It is no great feat for a naive imagination to suppose the President of the Swiss Confederation or the President of the United

States—for each of these two systems is an exemplary and encouraging instance of the possibility of the pacific synthesis of independent States—taking a propagandist course and proposing extensions of their own systems to the suffering belligerents.

But nothing of the sort occurs. And when you come to look into the circumstances of these two Presidents you will discover that neither of them is any more free than anybody else to embark upon the task of creating a State-overriding, war-preventing organisation of the world. He has been created by a system, and he is bound to a system; his concern is with the interests of the people of Switzerland or of the United States of America. President Wilson, for example, is quite sufficiently occupied by the affairs of the White House, by the clash of political parties, by interferences with American overseas trade and the security of American citizens. He has no more time to give to projects for the fundamental reconstruction of international relationships than has any recruit drilling in England, or any captain on an ocean liner, or any engineer in charge of a going engine.

We are all, indeed, busy with the things that come to hand every day. We are all anxious for a permanent world peace, but we are all up to the neck in things that leave us no time to attend to this world peace that nearly every sane man desires.

Meanwhile, a small minority of people who trade upon contention—militarists, ambitious kings and statesmen, war contractors, loan mongers, sensational journalists—follow up their interests and start and sustain war.

There lies the paradoxical reality of this question. Our first inquiry lands us into the elucidation of this deadlock. Nearly everybody desires a world peace, and yet there is not apparent anywhere any man free and able and willing to establish it, while, on the other hand, there are a considerable number of men in positions of especial influence and power who will certainly resist the arrangements that are essential to its establishment.

But does this exhaust the question, and must we conclude that mankind is doomed to a perpetual, futile struggling of States and nations and peoples—breaking ever and again into war? The answer to that would probably, be "Yes" if it were not for the progress of war. War is continually becoming more scientific, more destructive, more coldly logical, more intolerant of non-combatants, and more exhausting of any kind of property. There is every reason to believe that it will continue to intensify these characteristics. By doing so it may presently bring about a state of affairs that will supply just the lacking elements that are needed for the development of a world peace.

I would venture to suggest that the present war is doing so now: that it is producing changes in men's minds that may presently give us both the needed energy and the needed organisation from which a world direction may develop.

The first, most distinctive thing about this conflict is the exceptionally searching way in which it attacks human happiness. No war has ever destroyed happiness so widely. It has not only killed and wounded an unprecedented proportion of the male population of all the combatant nations, but it has also destroyed wealth beyond precedent. It has also destroyed freedom—of movement, of speech, of economic enterprise. Hardly anyone alive has escaped the worry of it and the threat of it. It has left scarcely a life untouched, and made scarcely a life happier. There is a limit to the principle that "everybody's business is nobody's business." The establishment of a world State, which was interesting only to a few cranks and visionaries before the war, is now the lively interest of a very great number of people. They inquire about it; they have become accessible to ideas about it.

Peace organisation seems, indeed, to be following the lines of public sanitation. Everybody in England, for example, was bored by the discussion of sanitation—until the great cholera epidemic. Everybody thought public health a very desirable thing, but nobody thought it intensely and overridingly desirable. Then the interest in sanitation grew lively, and people exerted themselves to create responsible organisations. Crimes of violence, again, were neglected in the great cities of Europe until the danger grew to dimensions that evolved the police. There come occasions when the normal concentration of an individual upon his own immediate concerns becomes impossible; as, for instance, when a man who is stocktaking in his business premises discovers that the house next door is on fire. A great many people who have never troubled their heads about anything but their own purely personal and selfish interests are now realising that quite a multitude of houses about them are ablaze, and that the fire is spreading.

That is one change the war will bring about that will make for world peace: a quickened general interest in its possibility. Another is the certainty that the war will increase the number of devoted and fanatic characters available for disinterested effort. Whatever other outcome this war may have, it means that there lies ahead a period of extreme economic and political dislocation. The credit system has been strained, and will be strained, and will need unprecedented readjustments. In the past such phases of uncertainty, sudden impoverishment and disorder as certainly lie ahead of us, have meant for a considerable number of minds a release—or, if you prefer it, a flight—from the habitual and selfish. Types of intense religiosity, of devotion and of endeavour are let loose, and there will be much more likelihood that we may presently find, what it is impossible to find now, a number of devoted men and women ready to give their whole lives, with a quasi-religious enthusiasm, to this great task of peace establishment, finding in such impersonal work a refuge from the disappoint-ments, limitations, losses and sorrows of their personal life—a refuge we need but little in more settled and more prosperous periods. They will be but the outstanding individuals in a very universal quickening. And simultaneously with this quickening of the general imagination by experience there are certain other developments in progress that point very clearly to a change under the pressure of this war of just those institutions of nationality, kingship, diplomacy and inter-State competition that have hitherto stood most effectually in the way of a world pacification. The considerations that seem to point to this third change are very convincing, to my mind.

The real operating cause that is, I believe, going to break down the deadlock that has hitherto made a supreme court and a federal government for the world at large a dream, lies in just that possibility of an "inconclusive peace" which so many people seem to dread. Germany, I believe, is going to be beaten, but not completely crushed, by this war; she is going to be left militarist and united with Austria and Hungary, and unchanged in her essential nature; and out of that state of affairs comes, I believe, the hope for an ultimate confederation of the nations of the earth.

Because, in the face of a league of the Central European Powers attempting recuperation, cherishing revenge, dreaming of a renewal of the struggle, it becomes impossible for the British, the French, the Belgians, Russians, Italians or Japanese to think any longer of settling their differences by war among themselves. To do so will mean the creation of opportunity for the complete reinstatement of German militarism. It will open the door for a conclusive German hegemony. Now, however clumsy and confused the diplomacy of these present Allies may be (challenged constantly, as it is, by democracy and hampered by a free, venal and irresponsible Press in at least three of their countries), the necessity they will be under will be so urgent and so evident, that it is impossible to imagine that they will not set up some permanent organ for the direction and co-ordination of their joint international relationships. It may be a queerly constituted body at first; it may be of a merely diplomatic pretension; it may be called a Congress, or any old name of that sort, but essentially its business will be to conduct a joint fiscal, military and naval policy, to keep the peace in the Balkans and Asia, to establish a relationship with China, and organise joint and several arbitration arrangements with America. And it must develop something more sure and swift than our present diplomacy. One of its chief concerns will be the right of way through the Bosphorus and the Dardanelles, and the watching of the forces that stir up conflict in the Balkans and the Levant. It must have unity enough for that; it must be much more than a mere leisurely, unauthoritative conference of representatives.

For precisely similar reasons it seems to me incredible that the two great Central European Powers should ever fall into sustained conflict again with one another. They, too, will be forced to create some overriding body to prevent so suicidal a possibility. America too, it may be, will develop some Pan-American equivalent. Probably the hundred millions of Latin America may achieve a method of unity, and then deal on equal terms with the present United States. The thing has been ably advocated already in South America. Whatever appearances of separate sovereignties are kept up after the war, the practical outcome of the struggle is quite likely to be this: that there will be only three great World Powers left—the anti-German allies, the allied Central Europeans, the Pan-Americans. And it is to be noted that, whatever the constituents of these three Powers may be, none of them is likely to be a monarchy. They may include monarchies, as England includes dukedoms. But they will be overriding alliances, not overriding rulers. I leave it to the mathematician to work out exactly how much the chances of conflict are diminished when there are practically only three Powers in the world instead of some scores. And these new Powers will be in certain respects unlike any existing European "States." None of the three Powers will be small or homogeneous enough to serve dynastic ambitions, embody a national or racial Kultur, or fall into the grip of any group of financial enterprises. They will be more comprehensive, less romantic, and more businesslike altogether. They will be, to use a phrase suggested a year or so ago, Great States.... And the war threat between the three will be so plain and definite, the issues will be so lifted out of the spheres of merely personal ambition and national feeling, that I do not see why the negotiating means, the standing conference of the three, should not ultimately become the needed nucleus of the World State for which at present we search the world in vain.

There are more ways than one to the World State, and this second possibility of a post-war conference and a conference of the Allies, growing almost unawares into a pacific organisation of the world, since it goes on directly from existing institutions, since it has none of the quality of a clean break with the past which the idea of an immediate World State and Pax Mundi involves, and more particularly since it neither abolishes nor has in it anything to shock fundamentally the princes, the diplomatists, the lawyers, the statesmen and politicians, the nationalists and suspicious people, since it gives them years in which to change and die out and reappear in new forms, and since at the same time it will command the support of every intelligent human being who gets his mind clear enough from his circumstances to understand its import, is a far more credible hope than the hope of anything coming *de novo* out of Hague Foundations or the manifest logic of the war.

But, of course, there weighs against these hopes the possibility that the Allied Powers are too various in their nature, too biased, too feeble intellectually and imaginatively, to hold together and maintain any institution for co-operation. The British Press may be too silly not to foster irritation and suspicion; we may get Carsonism on a larger scale trading on the resuscitation of dying hatreds; the British and Russian diplomatists may play annoying tricks upon one another by sheer force of habit. There may be many troubles of that sort. Even then I do not see that the hope of an ultimate world peace vanishes. But it will be a Roman world peace, made in Germany, and there will have to be several more great wars before it is established. Germany is too homogeneous yet to have begun the lesson of compromise and the renunciation of the dream of national conquest. The Germans are a national, not an imperial people. France has learnt that through suffering, and Britain and Russia because for two centuries they have been imperial and not national systems. The German conception of world peace is as yet a conception of German ascendancy. The Allied conception becomes perforce one of mutual toleration.

But I will not press this inquiry farther now. It is, as I said at the beginning, a preliminary exploration of one of the great questions with which I propose to play in these articles. The possibility I have sketched is the one that most commends itself to me as probable. After a more detailed examination of the big operating forces at present working in the world, we may be in a position to revise these suggestions with a greater confidence and draw our net of probabilities a little tighter.

II

THE END OF THE WAR[1]

The prophet who emerges with the most honour from this war is Bloch. It must be fifteen or sixteen years ago since this gifted Pole made his forecast of the future. Perhaps it is more, for the French translation of his book was certainly in existence before the Boer War. His case was that war between antagonists of fairly equal equipment must end in a deadlock because of the continually increasing defensive efficiency of entrenched infantry. This would give the defensive an advantage over the most brilliant strategy and over considerably superior numbers that would completely discourage all aggression. He concluded that war was played out.

[Footnote 1: This chapter was originally a newspaper article. It was written in December, 1915, and published about the middle of January. Some of it has passed from the quality of anticipation to achievement, but I do not see that it needs any material revision on that account.]

His book was very carefully studied in Germany. As a humble disciple of Bloch I should have realised this, but I did not, and that failure led me into some unfortunate prophesying at the outbreak of the war. I judged Germany by the Kaiser, and by the Kaiser-worship which I saw in Berlin. I thought that he was a theatrical person who would dream of vast massed attacks and tremendous cavalry charges, and that he would lead Germany to be smashed against the Allied defensive in the

West, and to be smashed so thoroughly that the war would be over. I did not properly appreciate the more studious and more thorough Germany that was to fight behind the Kaiser and thrust him aside, the Germany we British fight now, the Ostwald-Krupp Germany of 1915. That Germany, one may now perceive, had read and thought over and thought out the Bloch problem.

There was also a translation of Bloch into French. In English a portion of his book was translated for the general reader and published with a preface by the late Mr. W.T. Stead. It does not seem to have reached the British military authorities, nor was it published in England with an instructive intention. As an imaginative work it would have been considered worthless and impracticable.

But it is manifest now that if the Belgian and French frontiers had been properly prepared—as they should have been prepared when the Germans built their strategic railways—with trenches and gun emplacements and secondary and tertiary lines, the Germans would never have got fifty miles into either France or Belgium. They would have been held at Liege and in the Ardennes. Five hundred thousand men would have held them indefinitely. But the Allies had never worked trench warfare; they were unready for it, Germans knew of their unreadiness, and their unreadiness it is quite clear they calculated. They did not reckon, it is now clear that they were right in not reckoning, the Allies as contemporary soldiers. They were going to fight a 1900 army with a 1914 army, and their whole opening scheme was based on the conviction that the Allies would not entrench.

Somebody in those marvellous maxims from the dark ages that seem to form the chief reading of our military experts, said that the army that entrenches is a defeated army. The silly dictum was repeated and repeated in the English papers after the battle of the Marne. It shows just where our military science had reached in 1914, namely, to a level a year before Bloch wrote. So the Allies retreated.

For long weeks the Allies retreated out of the west of Belgium, out of the north of France, and for rather over a month there was a loose mobile war—as if Bloch had never existed. The Germans were not fighting the 1914 pattern of war, they were fighting the 1899 pattern of war, in which direct attack, outflanking and so on were still supposed to be possible; they were fighting confident in their overwhelming numbers, in their prepared surprise, in the unthought-out methods of their opponents. In the "Victorian" war that ended in the middle of September, 1914, they delivered their blow, they over-reached, they were successfully counter-attacked on the Marne, and then abruptly—almost unfairly it seemed to the British sportsmanlike conceptions—they shifted to the game played according to the very latest rules of 1914. The war did not come up to date until the battle of the Aisne. With that the second act of the great drama began.

I do not believe that the Germans ever thought it would come up to date so soon. I believe they thought that they would hustle the French out of Paris, come right up to the Channel at Calais before the end of 1914, and then entrench, produce the submarine attack and the Zeppelins against England, working from Calais as a base, and that they would end the war before the spring of 1915—with the Allies still a good fifteen years behindhand.

I believe the battle of the Marne was the decisive battle of the war, in that it shattered this plan, and that the rest of the 1914 fighting was Germany's attempt to reconstruct their broken scheme in the face of an enemy who was continually getting more and more nearly up to date with the fighting. By December, Bloch, who had seemed utterly discredited in August, was justified up to the hilt. The world was entrenched at his feet. By May the lagging military science of the British had so far overtaken events as to realise that shrapnel was no longer so important as high explosive, and within a year the significance of machine guns, a significance thoroughly venti-lated by imaginative writers fifteen years before, was being grasped by the conservative but by no means inadaptable leaders of Britain.

The war since that first attempt—admirably planned and altogether justifiable (from a military point of view, I mean)—of Germany to "rush" a victory, has consisted almost entirely of failures on both sides either to get round or through or over the situation foretold by Bloch. There has been only one marked success, the German success in Poland due to the failure of the Russian munitions. Then for a time the war in the East was mobile and precarious while the Russians retreated to their present positions, and the Germans pursued and tried to surround them. That was a lapse into the pre-Bloch style. Now the Russians are again entrenched, their supplies are restored, the Germans have a lengthened line of supplies, and Bloch is back upon his pedestal so far as the Eastern theatre goes.

Bloch has been equally justified in the Anglo-French attempt to get round through Gallipoli. The forces of the India Office have pushed their way through unprepared country towards Bagdad, and are now entrenching in Mesopotamia, but from the point of view of the main war that is too remote to be considered either getting through or getting round; and so too the losses of the German colonies and the East African War are scarcely to be reckoned with in the main war. They have no determining value. There remains the Balkan struggle. But the Balkan struggle is something else; it is something new. It must be treated separately. It is a war of treacheries and brags and appearances. It is not a part of, it is a sequence to, the deadlock war of 1915.

But before dealing with this new development of the latter half of 1915 it is necessary to consider certain general aspects of the deadlock war. It is manifest that the Germans hoped to secure an effective victory in this war before they ran up against Bloch. But reckoning with Bloch, as they certainly did, they hoped that even in the event of the war getting to earth, it would still be possible to produce novelties that would sufficiently neutralise Bloch to secure a victorious peace. With unexpectedly powerful artillery suddenly concentrated, with high explosives, with asphyxiating gas, with a well-organised system of grenade throwing and mining, with attacks of flaming gas, and above all with a vast munition-making plant to keep them going, they had a very reasonable chance of hacking their way through.

Against these prepared novelties the Allies have had to improvise, and on the whole the improvisation has kept pace with the demands made upon it. They have brought their military science up to date, and to-day the disparity in science and equipment between the antagonists has greatly diminished. There has been no escaping Bloch after all, and the deadlock, if no sudden peace occurs, can end now in only one thing, the exhaustion in various degrees of all the combatants and the succumbing of the most exhausted. The idea of a conclusive end of the traditional pattern to this war, of a triumphal entry into London, Paris, Berlin or Moscow, is to be dismissed altogether from our calculations. The end of this war will be a matter of negotiation between practically immobilized and extremely shattered antagonists.

There is, of course, one aspect of the Bloch deadlock that the Germans at least have contemplated. If it is not possible to get through or round, it may still be possible to get over. There is the air path.

This idea has certainly taken hold of the French mind, but France has been too busy and is temperamentally too economical to risk large expenditures upon what is necessarily an experiment. The British are too conservative and sceptical to be the pioneers in any such enterprise. The Russians have been too poor in the necessary resources of mechanics and material.

The Germans alone have made any sustained attempt to strike through the air at their enemies beyond the war zone. Their Zeppelin raids upon England have shown a steadily increasing efficiency, and it is highly probable that they will be repeated on a much larger scale before the war is over. Quite possibly, too, the Germans are developing an accessory force of large aeroplanes to co-operate in such an attack. The long coasts of Britain, the impossibility of their being fully equipped throughout their extent, except at a prohibitive cost of men and material, to resist air invaders, exposes the whole length of the island to considerable risk and annoyance from such an expedition.

It is doubtful, though, if the utmost damage an air raid is likely to inflict upon England would count materially in the exhaustion process, and the moral effect of these raids has been, and will be, to stiffen the British resolution to fight this war through to the conclusive ending of any such possibilities.

The net result of these air raids is an inflexible determination of the British people rather to die in death grips with German militarism than to live and let it survive. The best chance for the aircraft was at the beginning of the war, when a surprise development might have had astounding results. That chance has gone by. The Germans are racially inferior to both French and English in the air, and the probability of effective blows over the deadlock is on the whole a probability in favour of the Allies. Nor is there anything on or under the sea that seems likely now to produce decisive results. We return from these considerations to a strengthened acceptance of Bloch.

The essential question for the prophet remains therefore the question of which group of Powers will exhaust itself most rapidly. And following on from that comes the question of how the successive stages of exhaustion will manifest themselves in the combatant nations. The problems of this war, as of all war, end as they begin in national psychology.

But it will be urged that this is reckoning without the Balkans. I submit that the German thrust through the wooded wilderness of Serbia is really no part of the war that has ended in the deadlock of 1915. It is dramatic, tragic, spectacular, but it is quite inconclusive. Here there is no way round or through to any vital centre of Germany's antagonists. It turns nothing; it opens no path to Paris, London, or Petrograd. It is a long, long way from the Danube to either Egypt or Mesopotamia, and there—and there—Bloch is waiting. I do not think the Germans have any intention of so generous an extension of their responsibilities. The Balkan complication is no solution of the deadlock problem. It is the opening of the sequel.

A whole series of new problems are opened up directly we turn to this most troubled region of the Balkans—problems of the value of kingship, of nationality, of the destiny of such cities as Constantinople, which from their very beginning have never had any sort of nationality at all, of the destiny of countries such as Albania, where a tangle of intense tribal nationalities is distributed in spots and patches, or Dalmatia, where one extremely self-conscious nation and language is present in the towns and another in the surrounding country, or Asia Minor, where no definite national boundaries, no religious, linguistic, or social homogeneities have ever established themselves since the Roman legions beat them down.

But all these questions can really be deferred or set aside in our present discussion, which is a discussion of the main war. Whatever surprises or changes this last phase of the Eastern Empire, that blood-clotted melodrama, may involve, they will but assist and hasten on the essential conclusion of the great war, that the Central Powers and their pledged antagonists are in a deadlock, unable to reach a decision, and steadily, day by day, hour by hour, losing men, destroying material, spending credit, approaching something unprecedented, unknown, that we try to express to ourselves by the word exhaustion.

Just how the people who use the word "exhaustion" so freely are prepared to define it, is a matter for speculation. The idea seems to be a phase in which the production of equipped forces ceases through the using up of men or material or both. If the exhaustion is fairly mutual, it need not be decisive for a long time. It may mean simply an ebb of vigour on both sides, unusual hardship, a general social and economic

H. G. Wells

disorganisation and grading down. The fact that a great killing off of men is implicit in the process, and that the survivors will be largely under discipline, militates against the idea that the end may come suddenly through a vigorous revolutionary outbreak. Exhaustion is likely to be a very long and very thorough process, extending over years. A "war of attrition" may last into 1918 or 1919, and may bring us to conditions of strain and deprivation still only very vaguely imagined. What happens in the Turkish Empire or India or America or elsewhere may extend the areas of waste and accelerate or retard the process, but is quite unlikely to end it.

Let us ask now which of the combatants is likely to undergo exhaustion most rapidly, and what is of equal or greater importance, which is likely to feel it first and most? No doubt there is a bias in my mind, but it seems to me that the odds are on the whole heavily against the Central Powers. Their peculiar German virtue, their tremendously complete organisation, which enabled them to put so large a proportion of their total resources into their first onslaught and to make so great and rapid a recovery in the spring of 1915, leaves them with less to draw upon now. Out of a smaller fortune they have spent a larger sum. They are blockaded to a very considerable extent, and against them fight not merely the resources of the Allies, but, thanks to the complete British victory in the sea struggle, the purchasable resources of all the world.

Conceivably the Central Powers will draw upon the resources of their Balkan and Asiatic allies, but the extent to which they can do that may very easily be over-estimated. There is a limit to the power for treason of these supposititious German monarchs that Western folly has permitted to possess these Balkan thrones—thrones which need never have been thrones at all—and none of the Balkan peoples is likely to witness with enthusiasm the complete looting of its country in the German interest by a German court. Germany will have to pay on the nail for most of her Balkan help. She will have to put more into the Balkans than she takes out.

Compared with the world behind the Allies the Turkish Empire is a country of mountains, desert and undeveloped lands. To develop these regions into a source of supplies under the strains and shortages of war-time, will be an immense and dangerous undertaking for Germany. She may open mines she may never work, build railways that others will enjoy, sow harvests for alien reaping. The people the Bulgarians want in Bulgaria are not Germans but Bulgarians; the people the Turks want in Anatolia are not Germans but Turks. And for all these tasks Germany must send men. Men?

At present, so far as any judgment is possible, Germany is feeling the pinch of the war much more even than France, which is habitually parsimonious, and instinctively cleverly economical, and Russia, which is hardy and insensitive. Great Britain has really only begun to feel the stress. She has probably suffered economically no more than have Holland or Switzerland, and Italy and Japan have certainly suffered less. All these three great countries are still full of men, of gear, of saleable futures. In every part of the globe Great Britain has colossal investments. She has still to apply the great principle of conscription not only to her sons but to the property of her overseas investors and of her landed proprietors. She has not even looked yet at the German financial expedients of a year ago. She moves reluctantly, but surely, towards such a thoroughness of mobilisation. There need be no doubt that she will completely socialise herself, completely reorganise her whole social and economic structure sooner than lose this war. She will do it clumsily and ungracefully, with much internal bickering, with much trickery on the part of her lawyers, and much baseness on the part of her landlords; but she will do it not so slowly as a logical mind might anticipate. She will get there a little late, expensively, but still in time....

The German group, I reckon, therefore, will become exhausted first. I think, too, that Germany will, as a nation, feel and be aware of what is happening to her sooner than any other of the nations that are sharing in this process of depletion. In 1914 the Germans were reaping the harvest of forty years of

H. G. Wells

economic development and business enterprise. Property and plenty were new experiences, and a generation had grown up in whose world a sense of expansion and progress was normal. There existed amongst it no tradition of the great hardship of war, such as the French possessed, to steel its mind. It had none of the irrational mute toughness of the Russians and British. It was a sentimental people, making a habit of success; it rushed chanting to war against the most grimly heroic and the most stolidly enduring of races. Germany came into this war more buoyantly and confidently than any other combatant. It expected another 1871; at the utmost it anticipated a year of war.

Never were a people so disillusioned as the Germans must already be, never has a nation been called upon for so complete a mental readjustment. Neither conclusive victories nor defeats have been theirs, but only a slow, vast transition from joyful effort and an illusion of rapid triumph to hardship, loss and loss and loss of substance, the dwindling of great hopes, the realisation of ebb in the tide of national welfare. Now they must fight on against implacable, indomitable Allies. They are under stresses now as harsh at least as the stresses of France. And, compared with the French, the Germans are untempered steel.

We know little of the psychology of this new Germany that has come into being since 1871, but it is doubtful if it will accept defeat, and still more doubtful how it can evade some ending to the war that will admit the failure of all its great hopes of Paris subjugated, London humbled, Russia suppliant, Belgium conquered, the Near East a prey. Such an admission will be a day of reckoning that German Imperialism will postpone until the last hope of some breach among the Allies, some saving miracle in the old Eastern Empire, some dramatically-snatched victory at the eleventh hour, is gone.

Nor can the Pledged Allies consent to a peace that does not involve the evacuation and compensation of Belgium and Serbia, and at least the autonomy of the lost Rhine provinces of France. That is their very minimum. That, and the making of Germany so sick and weary of military adventure that the danger of German ambition will cease to overshadow European life. Those are the ends of the main war. Europe will go down through stage after stage of impoverishment and exhaustion until these ends are attained, or made for ever impossible.

But these things form only the main outline of a story with a vast amount of collateral interest. It is to these collateral issues that the amateur in prophecy must give his attention. It is here that the German will be induced by his Government to see his compensations. He will be consoled for the restoration of Serbia by the prospect of future conflicts between Italian and Jugoslav that will let him in again to the Adriatic. His attention will be directed to his newer, closer association with Bulgaria and Turkey. In those countries he will be told he may yet repeat the miracle of Hungary. And there may be also another Hungary in Poland. It will be whispered to him that he has really conquered those countries when indeed it is highly probable he has only spent his substance in setting up new assertive alien allies. The Kaiser, if he is not too afraid of the precedent of Sarajevo, may make a great entry into Constantinople, with an effect of conquering what is after all only a temporarily allied capital. The German will hope also to retain his fleet, and no peace, he will be reminded, can rob him of his hard-earned technical superiority in the air. The German air fleet of 1930 may yet be something as predominant as the British Navy of 1915, and capable of delivering a much more intimate blow. Had he not better wait for that? When such consolations as these become popular in the German Press we of the Pledged Allies may begin to talk of peace, for these will be its necessary heralds.

The concluding phase of a process of general exhaustion must almost inevitably be a game of bluff. Neither side will admit its extremity. Neither side, therefore, will make any direct proposals to its antagonists nor any open advances to a neutral. But there will be much inspired peace talk through neutral media, and the consultations of the anti-German allies will become more intimate and detailed. Suggestions will "leak out" remarkably from both sides, to journalists and neutral go-betweens. The Eastern and Western Allies will probably begin quite soon to discuss an anti-German Zollverein and the co-ordination of their military and naval organisations in the days that are to follow the war. A discussion of a Central European Zollverein is already afoot. A general idea of the possible rearrangement of the European States after the war will grow up in the common European and American mind; public men on either side will indicate concordance with this general idea, and some neutral power, Denmark or Spain or the United States or Holland, will invite representatives to an informal discussion of these possibilities.

Probably, therefore, the peace negotiations will take the extraordinary form of two simultaneous conferences—one of the Pledged Allies, sitting probably in Paris or London, and the other of representatives of all the combatants meeting in some neutral country—Holland would be the most convenient—while the war will still be going on. The Dutch conference would be in immediate contact by telephone and telegraph with the Allied conference and with Berlin....

The broad conditions of a possible peace will begin to get stated towards the end of 1916, and a certain lassitude will creep over the operations in the field.... The process of exhaustion will probably have reached such a point by that time that it will be a primary fact in the consciousness of common citizens of every belligerent country. The common life of all Europe will have become—miserable. Conclusive blows will have receded out of the imagination of the contending Powers. The war will have reached its fourth and last stage as a war. The war of the great attack will have given place to the war of the military deadlock; the war of the deadlock will have gone on, and as the great combatants have become enfeebled relatively to the smaller States, there will have been a gradual shifting of the interest to the war of treasons and diplomacies in the Eastern Mediterranean.

Quickly thereafter the last phase will be developing into predominance, in which each group of nations will be most concerned, no longer about victories or conquests, but about securing for itself the best chances of rapid economic recuperation and social reconstruction. The commercial treaties, the arrangements for future associated action, made by the great Allies among themselves will appear more and more important to them, and the mere question of boundaries less and less. It will dawn upon Europe that she has already dissipated the resources that have enabled her to levy the tribute paid for her investments in every quarter of the earth, and that neither the Germans nor their antagonists will be able for many years to go on with those projects for world exploitation which lay at the root of the great war. Very jaded and anaemic nations will sit about the table on which the new map of Europe will be drawn.... Each of the diplomatists will come to that business with a certain pre-occupation. Each will be thinking of his country as one thinks of a patient of doubtful patience and temper who is coming-to out of the drugged stupor of a crucial, ill-conceived, and unnecessary operation ... Each will be thinking of Labour, wounded and perplexed, returning to the disorganised or nationalised factories from which Capital has gone a-fighting, and to which it may never return.

III

NATIONS IN LIQUIDATION

The war has become a war of exhaustion. One hears a great deal of the idea that "financial collapse" may bring it to an end. A number of people seem to be convinced that a war cannot be waged without money, that soldiers must be paid, munitions must be bought; that for this money is necessary and the consent of bank depositors; so that if all the wealth of the world were nominally possessed by some one man in a little office he could stop the war by saying simply, "I will lend you no more money."

Now, as a matter of fact, money is a power only in so far as people believe in it and Governments sustain it. If a State is sufficiently strong and well organised, its control over the money power is unlimited. If it can rule its people, and if it has the necessary resources of men and material within its borders, it can go on in a state of war so long as these things last, with almost any flimsy sort of substitute for money that it chooses to print. It can enrol and use the men, and seize and work the material. It can take over the land and cultivate it and distribute its products. The little man in the office is only a power because the State chooses to recognise his claim. So long as he is convenient he seems to be a power. So soon as the State is intelligent enough and strong enough it can do without him. It can take what it wants, and tell him to go and hang himself. That is the melancholy ultimate of the usurer. That is the quintessence of "finance." All credit is State-made, and what the State has made the State can alter or destroy.

The owner and the creditor have never had any other power to give or withhold credit than the credit that was given to them. They exist by sufferance or superstition and not of necessity.

It is the habit of overlooking this little flaw in the imperatives of ownership that enables people to say that this war cannot go on beyond such and such a date—the end of 1916 is much in favour just now—because we cannot pay for it. It would be about as reasonable to expect a battle to end because a landlord had ordered the soldiers off his estate. So long as there are men to fight and stuff to fight with the war can go on. There is bankruptcy, but the bankruptcy of States is not like the bankruptcy of individuals. There is no such thing among States as an undischarged bankrupt who is forbidden to carry on. A State may keep on going bankrupt indefinitely and still carry on. It will be the next step in our prophetic exercise to examine the differences between State bankruptcy and the bankruptcy of a subject of the State.

The belligerent Powers are approaching a phase when they will no longer be paying anything like twenty shillings in the pound. In a very definite sense they are not paying twenty shillings in the pound now. That is not going to stop the war, but it involves a string of consequences and possibilities of the utmost importance to our problem of what is coming when the war is over.

The exhaustion that will bring this war to its end at last is a process of destruction of men and material. The process of bankruptcy that is also going on is nothing of the sort. Bankruptcy destroys no concrete thing; it merely writes off a debt; it destroys a financial but not an economic reality. It is, in itself, a mental, not a physical fact. "A" owes "B" a debt; he goes bankrupt and pays a dividend, a fraction of his debt, and gets his discharge. "B's" feelings, as we novelists used to say, are "better imagined than described"; he does his best to satisfy himself that "A" can pay no more, and then "A" and "B" both go about their business again.

In England, if "A" is a sufficiently poor man not to be formidable, and has gone bankrupt on a small scale, he gets squeezed ferociously to extract the last farthing from him; he may find himself in jail and his home utterly smashed up. If he is a richer man, and has failed on a larger scale, our law is more sympathetic, and he gets off much more easily. Often his creditors find it advisable to arrange with him so that he will still carry on with his bankrupt concern. They find it is better to allow him to carry on than to smash him up.

There are countless men in the world living very comfortably indeed, and running businesses that were once their own property for their creditors. There are still more who have written off princely debts and do not seem to be a "ha'p'orth the worse." And their creditors have found a balm in time and philosophy. Bankruptcy is only painful and destructive to small people and helpless people; but then for them everything is painful and destructive; it can be a very light matter to big people; it may be almost painless to a State.

If England went bankrupt in the completest way to-morrow, and repudiated all its debts both as a nation and as a community of individuals, if it declared, if I may use a self-contradictory phrase, a permanent moratorium, there would be not an acre of ploughed land in the country, not a yard of cloth or a loaf of bread the less for that. There would be nothing material destroyed within the State. There would be no immediate convulsion. Use and wont would carry most people on some days before they even began to doubt whether So-and-so could pay his way, and whether there would be wages at the end of the week.

But people who lived upon rent or investments or pensions would presently be very busy thinking how they were going to get food when the butcher and baker insisted upon cash. It would be only with comparative slowness that the bulk of men would realise that a fabric of confidence and confident assumptions had vanished; that cheques and bank notes and token money and every sort of bond and scrip were worthless, that employers had nothing to pay with, shopkeepers no means of procuring stock, that metallic money was disappearing, and that a paralysis had come upon the community.

Such an establishment as a workhouse or an old-fashioned monastery, living upon the produce of its own farming and supplying all its own labour, would be least embarrassed amidst the general perplexity. For it would not be upon a credit basis, but a socialistic basis, a basis of direct reality, and its need for payments would be incidental. And land-owning peasants growing their own food would carry on, and small cultivating occupiers, who could easily fall back on barter for anything needed.

The mass of the population in such a country as England would, however, soon be standing about in hopeless perplexity and on the verge of frantic panic—although there was just as much food to be eaten, just as many houses to live in, and just as much work needing to be done. Suddenly the pots would be empty, and famine would be in the land, although the farms and butchers' shops were still well stocked. The general community would be like an automobile when the magneto fails. Everything would be there and in order, except for the spark of credit which keeps the engine working.

That is how quite a lot of people seem to imagine national bankruptcy: as a catastrophic jolt. It is a quite impossible nightmare of cessation. The reality is the completest contrast. All the belligerent countries of the world are at the present moment quietly, steadily and progressively going bankrupt, and the mass of people are not even aware of this process of insolvency.

An individual when he goes bankrupt is measured by the monetary standard of the country he is in; he pays five or ten or fifteen or so many shillings in the pound. A community in debt does something which is in effect the same, but in appearance rather different. It still pays a pound, but the purchasing power of the pound has diminished. This is what is happening all over the world to-day; there is a rise in prices. This is automatic national bankruptcy; unplanned, though perhaps not unforeseen. It is not a deliberate State act, but a consequence of the interruption of communications, the diversion of productive energy, the increased demand for many necessities by the Government and the general waste under war conditions.

At the beginning of this war England had a certain national debt; it has paid off none of that original debt; it has added to it tremendously; so far as money and bankers' records go it still owes and intends to pay that original debt; but if you translate the language of L.s.d. into realities, you will find that in loaves or iron or copper or hours of toil, or indeed in any reality except gold, it owes now, so far as that original debt goes, far less than it did at the outset. As the war goes on and the rise in prices continues, the subsequent borrowings and contracts are undergoing a similar bankrupt reduction. The attempt of the landlord of small weekly and annual properties to adjust himself to the new conditions by raising rents is being checked by legislation in Great Britain, and has been completely checked in France. The attempts of labour to readjust wages have been partially successful in spite of the eloquent protests of those great exponents of plain living, economy, abstinence, and honest, modest, underpaid toil, Messrs. Asquith, McKenna, and Runciman. It is doubtful if the rise in wages is keeping pace with the rise in prices. So far as it fails to do so the load is on the usual pack animal, the poor man.

The rest of the loss falls chiefly upon the creditor class, the people with fixed incomes and fixed salaries, the landlords, who have let at long leases, the people with pensions, endowed institutions, the Church, insurance companies, and the like. They are all being scaled down. They are all more able to stand scaling down than the proletarians.

Assuming that it is possible to bring up wages to the level of the higher prices, and that the rise in rents can be checked by legislation or captured by taxation, the rise in prices is, on the whole, a thing to the advantage of the propertyless man as against accumulated property. It writes off the past and clears the way for a fresh start in the future.

An age of cheapness is an old usurers' age. England before the war was a paradise of ancient usuries; everywhere were great houses and enclosed parks; the multitude of gentlemen's servants and golf clubs and such like excrescences of the comfort of prosperous people was perpetually increasing; it did not "pay" to build labourers' cottages, and the more expensive sort of automobile had driven the bicycle as a pleasure vehicle off the roads. Western Europe was running to fat and not to muscle, as America is to-day.

But if that old usurer's age is over, the young usurer's age may be coming. To meet such enormous demands as this war is making there are three chief courses open to the modern State.

The first is to *take*—to get men by conscription and material by requisition. The British Government *takes* more modestly than any other in the world; its tradition from Magna Charta onward, the legal training of most of its members, all make towards a reverence for private ownership and private claims, as opposed to the claims of State and commonweal, unequalled in the world's history.

The next course of a nation in need is to *tax* and pay for what it wants, which is a fractional and more evenly distributed method of taking. Both of these methods raise prices, the second most so, and so facilitate the automatic release of the future from the boarding of the past. So far all the belligerent Governments have taxed on the timid side.

Finally there is the *loan*. This mortgages the future to the present necessity, and it has so far been the predominant source of war credits. It is the method that produces least immediate friction in the State; it employs all the savings of surplus income that the unrest of civil enterprise leaves idle; it has an effect of creating property by a process that destroys the substance of the community. In Germany an enormous bulk of property has been mortgaged to supply the subscriptions to the war loans, and those holdings have again been hypothecated to subscribe to subsequent loans. The Pledged Allies with longer stockings have not yet got to this pitch of overlapping. But everywhere in Europe what is happening is a great transformation of the property owner into a *rentier*, and the passing of realty into the hands of the State.

At the end of the war Great Britain will probably find herself with a national debt so great that she will be committed to the payment of an annual interest greater in figures than the entire national expenditure before the war. As an optimistic lady put it the other day: "All the people who aren't killed will be living quite comfortably on War Loan for the rest of their lives."

But part, at least, of the bulk of this wealth will be imaginary rather than real because of the rise in prices, in wages, in rent, and in taxation. Most of us who are buying the British and French War Loans have no illusions on that score; we know we are buying an income of diminishing purchasing power. Yet it would be a poor creature in these days when there is scarcely a possible young man in one's circle who has not quite freely and cheerfully staked his life, who was not prepared to consider his investments as being also to an undefined extent a national subscription.

A rise in prices is not, however, the only process that will check the appearance of a new rich usurer class after the war. There is something else ahead that has happened already in Germany, that is quietly coming about among the Allies, and that is the cessation of gold payments. In Great Britain, of course, the pound note is still convertible into a golden sovereign; but Great Britain will not get through the war on those terms. There comes a point in the stress upon a Government when it must depart from the austerer line of financial rectitude—and tamper in some way with currency.

Sooner or later, and probably in all cases before 1917, all the belligerents will be forced to adopt inconvertible paper money for their internal uses. There will be British assignats or greenbacks. It will seem to many financial sentimentalists almost as though Great Britain were hauling down a flag when the sovereign, which has already disappeared into bank and Treasury coffers, is locked up there and reserved for international trade. But Great Britain has other sentiments to consider than the finer feelings of bankers and the delicacies of usury. The pound British will come out of this war like a company out of a well-shelled trench—attenuated.

Depreciation of the currency means, of course, a continuing rise in prices, a continuing writing off of debt. If labour has any real grasp of its true interests it will not resent this. It will merely insist steadfastly on a proper adjustment of its wages to the new standard. On that point, however, it will be better to write later....

Let us see how far we have got in this guessing. We have considered reasons that seem to point to the destruction of a great amount of old property and old debt, and the creation of a great volume of new debt before the end of the war, and we have adopted the ideas that currency will probably have depreciated more and more and prices risen right up to the very end.

There will be by that time a general habit of saving throughout the community, a habit more firmly established perhaps in the propertied than in the wages-earning class. People will be growing accustomed to a dear and insecure world. They will adopt a habit of caution; become desirous of saving and security.

Directly the phase of enormous war loans ends, the new class of *rentiers* holding the various great new national loans will find themselves drawing this collectively vast income and anxious to invest it. They will for a time be receiving the bulk of the unearned income of the world. Here, in the high prices representing demand and the need for some reinvestment of interest representing supply, we have two of the chief factors that are supposed to be necessary to a phase of business enterprise. Will the economic history of the next few decades be the story of a restoration of the capitalistic system upon a new basis? Shall we all become investors, speculators, or workers toiling our way to a new period of security, cheapness and low interest, a restoration of the park, the enclosure, the gold standard and the big automobile, with only this difference—that the minimum wage will be somewhere about two pounds, and that a five-pound note will purchase about as much as a couple of guineas would do in 1913?

That is practically parallel with what happened in the opening half of the nineteenth century after the Napoleonic wars, and it is not an agreeable outlook for those who love the common man or the nobility of life. But if there is any one principle sounder than another of all those that guide the amateur in prophecy, it is that *history never repeats itself.* The human material in which those monetary changes and those developments of credit will occur will be entirely different from the social medium of a hundred years ago.

The nature of the State has altered profoundly in the last century. The later eighteenth and earlier nineteenth centuries constituted a period of extreme individualism. What were called "economic forces" had unrestricted play. In the minds of such people as Harriet Martineau and Herbert Spencer they superseded God. People were no longer reproached for "flying in the face of Providence," but for "flying in the face of Political Economy."

In that state of freedom you got whatever you could in any way you could; you were not your neighbour's keeper, and except that it interfered with the enterprise of pickpockets, burglars and forgers, and kept the dice loaded in favour of landlords and lawyers, the State stood aside from the great drama of human getting. For industrialism and speculation the State's guiding maxim was *laissez faire.*

The State is now far less aloof and far more constructive. It is far more aware of itself and a common interest. Germany has led the way from a system of individuals and voluntary associations in competition towards a new order of things, a completer synthesis. This most modern State is far less a swarming conflict of businesses than a great national business. It will emerge from this war much more so than it went in, and the thing is and will remain so plain and obvious that only the greediest and dullest people among the Pledged Allies will venture to disregard it. The Allied nations, too, will have to rescue their economic future from individual grab and grip and chance.

The second consideration that forbids us to anticipate any parallelism of the history of 1915-45 with 1815-45 is the greater lucidity of the general mind, the fact that all Western Europe, down to the agricultural labourers, can read and write and does read newspapers and "get ideas." The explanation of economic and social processes that were mysterious to the elect a hundred years ago are now the commonplaces of the tap-room. What happened then darkly, and often unconsciously, must happen in 1916-26 openly and controllably. The current bankruptcy and liquidation and the coming reconstruction of the economic system of Europe will go on in a quite unprecedented amount of light. We shall see and know what is happening much more clearly than anything of the kind has ever been seen before.

It is not only that people will have behind them, as a light upon what is happening, the experiences and discussions of a hundred years, but that the international situation will be far plainer than it has ever been. This war has made Germany the central fact in all national affairs about the earth. It is not going to destroy Germany, and it seems improbable that either defeat or victory, or any mixture of these, will immediately alter the cardinal fact of Germany's organized aggressiveness.

The war will not end the conflict of anti-Germany and Germany, That will only end when the results of fifty years of aggressive education in Germany have worn away. This will be so plain that the great bulk of people everywhere will not only see their changing economic relationships far more distinctly than such things have been seen hitherto, but that they will see them as they have never been seen before, definitely orientated to the threat of German world predominance. The landlord who squeezes, the workman who strikes and shirks, the lawyer who fogs and obstructs, will know, and will know that most people know, that what he does is done, not under an empty, regardless heaven, but in the face of an unsleeping enemy and in disregard of a continuous urgent necessity for unity.

So far we have followed this speculation upon fairly firm ground, but now our inquiry must plunge into a jungle of far more difficult and uncertain possibilities. Our next stage brings us to the question of how people and peoples and classes of people are going to react to the new conditions of need and knowledge this war will have brought about, and to the new demands that will be made upon them.

This is really a question of how far they will prove able to get out of the habits and traditions of their former social state, how far they will be able to take generous views and make sacrifices and unselfish efforts, and how far they will go in self-seeking or class selfishness regardless of the common welfare. This is a question we have to ask separately of each great nation, and of the Central Powers as a whole, and of the Allies as a whole, before we can begin to estimate the posture of the peoples of the world in, say, 1946.

Now let me here make a sort of parenthesis on human nature. It will be rather platitudinous, but it is a necessary reminder for what follows.

So far as I have been able to observe, nobody lives steadily at one moral level. If we are wise we shall treat no man and no class—and for the matter of that no nation—as either steadfastly malignant or steadfastly disinterested. There are phases in my life when I could die quite cheerfully for an idea;

there are phases when I would not stir six yards to save a human life. Most people fluctuate between such extremes. Most people are self-seeking, but most people will desist from a self-seeking cause if they see plainly and clearly that it is not in the general interest, and much more readily if they also perceive that other people are of the same mind and know that they know their course is unsound.

The fundamental error of orthodox political economy and of Marxian socialism is to assume the inveterate selfishness of everyone. But most people are a little more disposed to believe what it is to their interest to believe than the contrary. Most people abandon with reluctance ways of living and doing that have served them well. Most people can see the neglect of duty in other classes more plainly than they do in their own.

This war has brought back into the everyday human life of Europe the great and overriding conception of devotion to a great purpose. But that does not imply clear-headedness in correlating the ways of one's ordinary life with this great purpose. It is no good treating as cynical villainy things that merely exhibit the incapacity of our minds to live consistently.

One Labour paper a month or so ago was contrasting Mr. Asquith's eloquent appeals to the working man to economise and forgo any rise in wages with the photographs that were appearing simultaneously in the smart papers of the very smart marriage of Mr. Asquith's daughter. I submit that by that sort of standard none of us will be blameless. But without any condemnation, it is easy to understand that the initiative to tax almost to extinction large automobiles, wedding dresses, champagne, pate de foie gras and enclosed parks, instead of gin and water, bank holiday outings and Virginia shag, is less likely to come from the Prime Minister class than from the class of dock labourers. There is an unconscious class war due to habit and insufficient thinking and insufficient sympathy that will play a large part in the distribution of the burthen of the State bankruptcy that is in progress, and in the subsequent readjustment of national life.

And having made this parenthesis, I may perhaps go on to point out the peculiar limitations under which various classes will be approaching the phase of reorganisation, without being accused of making this or that class the villain of an anticipatory drama.

Now, three great classes will certainly resist the valiant reconstruction of economic life with a vigour in exact proportion to their baseness, stupidity and narrowness of outlook. They will, as classes, come up for a moral judgment, on whose verdict the whole future of Western civilisation depends. If they cannot achieve a considerable, an unprecedented display of self-sacrifice, unselfish wisdom, and constructive vigour, if the community as a whole can produce no forces sufficient to restrain their lower tendencies, then the intelligent father had better turn his children's faces towards the New World. For Europe will be busy with social disorder for a century.

The first great class is the class that owns and holds land and land-like claims upon the community, from the Throne downward. This Court and land-holding class cannot go on being rich and living rich during the strains of the coming years. The reconstructing world cannot bear it. Whatever rises in rent may occur through the rise in prices, must go to meet the tremendous needs of the State.

This class, which has so much legislative and administrative power in at least three of the great belligerents—in Great Britain and Germany perhaps most so—must be prepared to see itself taxed, and must be willing to assist in its own taxation to the very limit of its statistical increment. The almost vindictive greed of the landowners that blackened the history of England after Waterloo, and brought Great Britain within sight of revolution, must not be repeated. The British Empire cannot afford a revolution in the face of the Central European Powers. But in the past century there has been an enormous change in men's opinions and consciences about property; whereas we were Individualists, now we are Socialists. The British lord, the German junker, has none of the sense of unqualified rights that his great-grandfather had, and he is aware of a vigour of public criticism that did not exist in the former time....

How far will these men get out of the tradition of their birth and upbringing?

Next comes the great class of lawyers who, through the idiotic method of voting in use in modern democracies, are able practically to rule Great Britain, and who are powerful and influential in all democratic countries.

In order to secure a certain independence and integrity in its courts, Great Britain long ago established the principle of enormously overpaying its judges and lawyers. The natural result has been to give our law courts and the legal profession generally a bias in favour of private wealth against both the public interest and the proletariat. It has also given our higher national education an overwhelming direction towards the training of advocates and against science and constructive statecraft. An ordinary lawyer has no idea of making anything; that tendency has been destroyed in his mind; he waits and sees and takes advantage of opportunity. Everything that can possibly be done in England is done to make our rulers Micawbers and Artful Dodgers.

One of the most anxious questions that a Briton can ask himself to-day is just how far the gigantic sufferings and still more monstrous warnings of this war have shocked the good gentlemen who must steer the ship of State through the strong rapids of the New Peace out of this forensic levity their training has imposed upon them....

There, again, there are elements of hope. The lawyer has heard much about himself in the past few years. His conscience may check his tradition. And we have a Press—it has many faults, but it is no longer a lawyer's Press....

And the third class which has immediate interests antagonistic to bold reconstructions of our national methods is that vaguer body, the body of investing capitalists, the savers, the usurers, who live on dividends. It is a vast class, but a feeble class in comparison with the other two; it is a body rather than a class, a weight rather than a power. It consists of all sorts of people with nothing in common except the receipt of unearned income....

All these classes, by instinct and the baser kinds of reason also, will be doing their best to check the rise in prices, stop and reverse the advance in wages, prevent the debasement of the circulation, and facilitate the return to a gold standard and a repressive social stability. They will be resisting any comprehensive national reconstruction, any increase in public officials, any "conscription" of land or railways or what not for the urgent civil needs of the State. They will have fighting against these tendencies something in their own consciences, something in public opinion, the tradition of public devotion their own dead sons have revived—and certain other forces.

They will have over against them the obvious urgent necessities of the time.

The most urgent necessity will be to get back the vast moiety of the population that has been engaged either in military service or the making of munitions to productive work, to the production of food and necessary things, and to the restoration of that export trade which, in the case of Great Britain at least, now that her overseas investments have been set off by overseas war debts, is essential to the food supply. There will be coming back into civil life, not merely thousands, but millions of men who have been withdrawn from it. They will feel that they have deserved well of their country. They will have had their imaginations greatly quickened by being taken away from the homes and habits to which they were accustomed. They will have been well fed and inured to arms, to danger, and the chances of death. They will have no illusions about the conduct of the war by the governing classes, or the worshipful heroism of peers and princes. They will know just how easy is courage, and how hard is hardship, and the utter impossibility of doing well in war or peace under the orders of detected fools.

This vast body will constitute a very stimulating congregation of spectators in any attempt on the part of landlord, lawyer and investor to resume the old political mystery dance, in which rents are to be sent up and wages down, while the old feuds of Wales and Ireland, ancient theological and sectarian jealousies and babyish loyalties, and so forth are to be waved in the eyes of the no longer fascinated realist.

"Meanwhile," they will say, with a stiff impatience unusual in their class, "about *us?*" ...

Here are the makings of internal conflict in every European country. In Russia the landlord and lawyer, in France the landlord, are perhaps of less account, and in France the investor is more universal and jealous. In Germany, where Junker and Court are most influential and brutal, there is a larger and sounder and broader tradition of practical efficiency, a modernised legal profession, and a more widely diffused scientific imagination.

How far in each country will imagination triumph over tradition and individualism? How far does the practical bank-ruptcy of Western civilisation mean a revolutionary smash-up, and a phase that may last for centuries, of disorder and more and more futile conflict? And how far does it mean a reconstruction of human society, within a few score of years, upon sounder and happier lines? Must that reconstruction be preceded by a revolution in all or any of the countries?

To what extent can the world produce the imagination it needs? That, so far, is the most fundamental question to which our prophetic explorations have brought us.

IV

BRAINTREE, BOCKING, AND THE
FUTURE OF THE WORLD

Will the war be followed by a period of great distress, social disorder and a revolution in Europe, or shall we pull through the crisis without violent disaster? May we even hope that Great Britain will step straight out of the war into a phase of restored and increasing welfare?

Like most people, I have been trying to form some sort of answer to this question. My state of mind in the last few months has varied from a considerable optimism to profound depression. I have met and talked to quite a number of young men in khaki—ex-engineers, ex-lawyers, ex-schoolmasters, ex-business men of all sorts—and the net result of these interviews has been a buoyant belief that there is in Great Britain the pluck, the will, the intelligence to do anything, however arduous and difficult, in the way of national reconstruction. And on the other hand there is a certain stretch of road between Dunmow and Coggeshall....

That stretch of road is continually jarring with my optimistic thoughts. It is a strongly pro-German piece of road. It supports allegations against Great Britain, as, for instance, that the British are quite unfit to control their own affairs, let alone those of an empire; that they are an incompetent people, a pig-headedly stupid people, a wasteful people; a people incapable of realising that a man who tills his field badly is a traitor and a weakness to his country....

Let me place the case of this high road through Braintree (Bocking intervening) before the reader. It is, you will say perhaps, very small beer. But a straw shows the way the wind blows. It is a trivial matter of road metal, mud, and water-pipes, but it is also diagnostic of the essential difficulties in the way of the smooth and rapid reconstruction of Great Britain— and very probably of the reconstruction of all Europe—after the war. The Braintree high road, I will confess, becomes at times an image of the world for me. It is a poor, spiritless-looking bit of road, with raw stones on one side of it. It is also, I perceive, the high destiny of man in conflict with mankind. It is the way to Harwich, Holland, Russia, China, and the whole wide world.

Even at the first glance it impresses one as not being the road that would satisfy an energetic and capable people. It is narrow for a high road, and in the middle of it one is checked by an awkward bend, by cross-roads that are not exactly cross-roads, so that one has to turn two blind corners to get on eastward, and a policeman, I don't know at what annual cost, has to be posted to nurse the traffic across. Beyond that point one is struck by the fact that the south side is considerably higher than the north, that storm water must run from the south side to the north and lie there. It does, and the north side has recently met the trouble by putting down raw flints, and so converting what would be a lake into a sort of flint pudding. Consequently one drives one's car as much as possible on the south side of this road. There is a suggestion of hostility and repartee between north and south side in this arrangement, which the explorer's inquiries will confirm. It may be only an accidental parallelism with profounder fact; I do not know. But the middle of this high road is a frontier. The south side belongs to the urban district of Braintree; the north to the rural district of Bocking.

If the curious inquirer will take pick and shovel he will find at any rate one corresponding dualism below the surface. He will

H. G. Wells

find a Bocking water main supplying the houses on the north side and a Braintree water main supplying the south. I rather suspect that the drains are also in duplicate. The total population of Bocking and Braintree is probably little more than thirteen thousand souls altogether, but for that there are two water supplies, two sets of schools, two administrations.

To the passing observer the rurality of the Bocking side is indistinguishable from the urbanity of the Braintree side; it is just a little muddier. But there are dietetic differences. If you will present a Bocking rustic with a tin of the canned fruit that is popular with the Braintree townsfolk, you discover one of these differences. A dustman perambulates the road on the Braintree side, and canned food becomes possible and convenient therefore. But the Braintree grocers sell canned food with difficulty into Bocking. Bocking, less fortunate than its neighbour, has no dustman apparently, and is left with the tin on its hands. It can either bury it in its garden—if it has a garden—take it out for a walk wrapped in paper and drop it quietly in a ditch, if possible in the Braintree area, or build a cairn with it and its predecessors and successors in honour of the Local Government Board (President L5,000, Parliamentary Secretary L1,500, Permanent Secretary L2,000, Legal Adviser L1,000 upward, a total administrative expenditure of over L300,000 ...). In death Bocking and Braintree are still divided. They have their separate cemeteries....

Now to any disinterested observer there lies about the Braintree-Bocking railway station one community. It has common industries and common interests. There is no *octroi* or anything of that sort across the street. The shops and inns on the Bocking side of the main street are indistinguishable from those on the Braintree side. The inhabitants of the two communities intermarry freely. If this absurd separation did not exist, no one would have the impudence to establish it now. It is wasteful, unfair (because the Bocking piece is rather better off than Braintree and with fewer people, so that there is a difference in the rates), and for nine-tenths of the community it is more or less of a nuisance.

It is also a nuisance to the passing public because of such inconvenience as the asymmetrical main road. It hinders local development and the development of a local spirit. It may, of course, appeal perhaps to the humorous outlook of the followers of Mr. G.K. Chesterton and Mr. Belloc, who believe that this war is really a war in the interests of the Athanasian Creed, fatness, and unrestricted drink against science, discipline, and priggishly keeping fit enough to join the army, as very good fun indeed, good matter for some jolly reeling ballad about Roundabout and Roundabout, the jolly town of Roundabout; but to anyone else the question of how it is that this wasteful Bocking-Braintree muddle, with its two boards, its two clerks, its two series of jobs and contracts, manages to keep on, was even before the war a sufficiently discouraging one.

It becomes now a quite crucial problem. Because the muddle between the sides of the main road through Bocking and Braintree is not an isolated instance; it is a fair sample of the way things are done in Great Britain; it is an intimation of the way in which the great task of industrial resettlement that the nation must face may be attempted.

It is—or shall I write, "it may be"?

That is just the question I do not settle in my mind. I would like to think that I have hit upon a particularly bad case of entangled local government. But it happens that whenever I have looked into local affairs I have found the same sort of waste and—insobriety of arrangement. When I started, a little while back, to go to Braintree to verify these particulars, I was held up by a flood across the road between Little Easton and Dunmow. Every year that road is flooded and impassable for some days, because a bit of the affected stretch is under the County Council and a bit under the Little Easton Parish Council, and they cannot agree about the contribution of the latter. These things bump against the most unworldly. And when one goes up the scale from the urban district and rural district boundaries, one finds equally crazy county arrangements, the same tangle of obstacle in the way of quick, effective co-ordinations, the same needless multiplicity of clerks, the same rich possibilities of litigation, misunderstanding, and deadlocks of opinion between areas whose only difference is that a mischievous boundary has been left in existence between them. And so on up to Westminster. And to still greater things....

I know perfectly well how unpleasant all this is to read, this outbreak at two localities that have never done me any personal harm except a little mud-splashing. But this is a thing that has to be said now, because we are approaching a crisis when dilatory ways, muddle, and waste may utterly ruin us. This is the way things have been done in England, this is our habit of procedure, and if they are done in this way after the war this Empire is going to smash.

Let me add at once that it is quite possible that things are done almost as badly or quite as badly in Russia or France or Germany or America; I am drawing no comparisons. All of us human beings were made, I believe, of very similar clay, and very similar causes have been at work everywhere. Only that excuse, so popular in England, will not prevent a smash if we stick to the old methods under the stresses ahead. I do not see that it is any consolation to share in a general disaster.

And I am sure that there must be the most delightful and picturesque reasons why we have all this overlapping and waste and muddle in our local affairs; why, to take another example, the boundary of the Essex parishes of Newton and Widdington looks as though it had been sketched out by a drunken man in a runaway cab with a broken spring.

This Bocking-Braintree main road is, it happens, an old Stane Street, along which Roman legions marched to clean up the councils and clerks of the British tribal system two thousand years ago, and no doubt an historian could spin delightful consequences; this does not alter the fact that these quaint complications in English affairs mean in the aggregate enormous obstruction and waste of human energy. It does not alter the much graver fact, the fact that darkens all my outlook upon the future, that we have never yet produced evidence of any general disposition at any time to straighten out or even suspend these fumbling intricacies and ineptitudes. Never so far has there appeared in British affairs that divine passion to do things in the clearest, cleanest, least wasteful, most thorough manner that is needed to straighten out, for example, these universal local tangles. Always we have been content with the old intricate, expensive way, and to this day we follow it....

And what I want to know, what I would like to feel much surer about than I do is, is this in our blood? Or is it only the deep-seated habit of long ages of security, long years of margins so ample, that no waste seemed altogether wicked. Is it, in fact, a hopeless and ineradicable trait that we stick to extravagance and confusion?

What I would like to think possible at the present time, up and down the scale from parish to province, is something of this sort. Suppose the clerk of Braintree went to the clerk of Bocking and said: "Look here, one of us could do the work of both of us, as well or better. The easy times are over, and offices as well as men should be prepared to die for their country. Shall we toss to see who shall do it, and let the other man go off to find something useful to do?" Then I could believe. Such acts of virtue happen in the United States. Here is a quotation from the New York *World* of February 15th, 1916:

"For two unusual acts Henry Bruere may be remembered by New York longer than nine days. Early in his incumbency he declared that his office was superfluous and should be abolished, the Comptroller assuming its duties. He now abolishes by resignation his own connection with it, in spite of its $12,000 salary."

Suppose the people of Braintree and Bocking, not waiting for that lead, said: "But this is absurd! Let us have an identical council and one clerk, and get ahead, instead of keeping up this silly pretence that one town is two." Suppose someone of that 300,000 pounds' worth of gentlemen at the Local Government Board set to work to replan our local government areas generally on less comic lines. Suppose his official superiors helped, instead of snubbing him....

I see nothing of the sort happening. I see everywhere wary, watchful little men, thinking of themselves, thinking of their parish, thinking close, holding tight....

I know that there is a whole web of excuses for all these complicated, wasteful, and obstructive arrangements of our local government, these arrangements that I have taken merely as a sample of the general human way of getting affairs done. For it is affairs at large I am writing about, as I warned the reader at the beginning. Directly one inquires closely into any human muddle, one finds all sorts of reasonable rights and objections and claims barring the way to any sweeping proposals. I can quite imagine that Bocking has admirable reasons for refusing coalescence with Braintree, except upon terms that Braintree could not possibly consider. I can quite understand that there are many inconveniences and arguable injustices that would be caused by a merger of the two areas. I have no doubt it would mean serious loss to So-and-so, and quite novel and unfair advantage to So-and-so. It would take years to work the thing and get down to the footing of one water supply and an ambidextrous dustman on the lines of perfect justice and satisfactoriness all round.

But what I want to maintain is that these little immediate claims and rights and vested interests and bits of justice and fairness are no excuse at all for preventing things being done in the clear, clean, large, quick way. They never constituted a decent excuse, and now they excuse waste and delay and inconvenience less than ever. Let us first do things in the sound way, and then, if we can, let us pet and compensate any disappointed person who used to profit by their being done roundabout instead of earning an honest living. We are beginning to agree that reasonably any man may be asked to die for his country; what we have to recognise is that any man's proprietorship, interest, claims or rights may just as properly be called upon to die. Bocking and Braintree and Mr. John Smith—Mr. John Smith, the ordinary comfortable man with a stake in the country—have been thinking altogether too much of the claims and rights and expectations and economies of Bocking and Braintree and Mr. John Smith. They have to think now in a different way....

Just consider the work of reconstruction that Great Britain alone will have to face in the next year or so. (And her task is, if anything, less than that of any of her antagonists or Allies, except Japan and Italy.) She has now probably from six to ten million people in the British Isles, men and women, either engaged directly in warfare or in the manufacture of munitions or in employments such as transit, nursing, and so forth, directly subserving these main ends. At least five-sixths of these millions must be got back to employment of a different character within a year of the coming of peace. Everywhere manufacture, trade and transit has been disorganised, disturbed or destroyed. A new economic system has to be put together within a brief score or so of weeks; great dislocated masses of population have to be fed, kept busy and distributed in a world financially strained and abounding in wounded, cripples, widows, orphans and helpless people.

In the next year or so the lives of half the population will have to be fundamentally readjusted. Here is work for administrative giants, work for which no powers can be excessive. It will be a task quite difficult enough to do even without the opposition of legal rights, haggling owners, and dexterous profiteers. It would be a giant's task if all the necessary administrative machinery existed now in the most perfect condition. How is this tremendous job going to be done if every Bocking in the country is holding out for impossible terms from Braintree, and every Braintree holding out for impossible terms from Bocking, while the road out remains choked and confused between them; and if every John Smith with a claim is insisting upon his reasonable expectation of profits or dividends, his reasonable solatium and compensation for getting out of the way?

I would like to record my conviction that if the business of this great crisis is to be done in the same spirit, the jealous, higgling, legal spirit that I have seen prevailing in British life throughout my half-century of existence, it will not in any satisfactory sense of the phrase get done at all. This war has greatly demoralised and discredited the governing class in Great Britain, and if big masses of unemployed and unfed people, no longer strung up by the actuality of war, masses now trained to arms and with many quite sympathetic officers available, are released clumsily and planlessly into a world of risen prices and rising rents, of legal obstacles and forensic complications, of greedy speculators and hampered enterprises, there will be insurrection and revolution. There will be bloodshed in the streets and the chasing of rulers.

There *will* be, if we do seriously attempt to put the new wine of humanity, the new crude fermentations at once so hopeful and so threatening, that the war has released, into the old administrative bottles that served our purposes before the war.

I believe that for old lawyers and old politicians and "private ownership" to handle the great problem of reconstruction after the war in the spirit in which our affairs were conducted before the war is about as hopeful an enterprise as if an elderly jobbing brick-layer, working on strict trade-union rules, set out to stop the biggest avalanche that ever came down a mountain-side. And since I am by no means altogether pessimistic, in spite of my qualmy phases, it follows that I do not believe that the old spirit will necessarily prevail. I do not, because I believe that in the past few decades a new spirit has come into human affairs; that our ostensible rulers and leaders have been falling behind the times, and that in the young and the untried, in, for example, the young European of thirty and under who is now in such multitudes thinking over life and his seniors in the trenches, there are still unsuspected resources of will and capacity, new mental possibilities and new mental habits, that entirely disturb the argument—based on the typical case of Bocking and Braintree—for a social catastrophe after the war.

How best can this new spirit be defined?

It is the creative spirit as distinguished from the legal spirit; it is the spirit of courage to make and not the spirit that waits and sees and claims; it is the spirit that looks to the future and not to the past. It is the spirit that makes Bocking forget that it is not Braintree and John Smith forget that he is John Smith, and both remember that they are England.

For everyone there are two diametrically different ways of thinking about life; there is individualism, the way that comes as naturally as the grunt from a pig, of thinking outwardly from oneself as the center of the universe, and there is the way that every religion is trying in some form to teach, of thinking back to oneself from greater standards and realities. There is the Braintree that is Braintree against England and the world, giving as little as possible and getting the best of the bargain, and there is the Braintree that identifies itself with England and asks how can we do best for the world with this little place of ours, how can we educate best, produce most, and make our roads straight and good for the world to go through.

Every American knows the district that sends its congressman to Washington for the good of his district, and the district, the rarer district, that sends a man to work for the United States. There is the John Smith who feels toward England and the world as a mite feels toward its cheese, and the John Smith who feels toward his country as a sheep-dog feels toward the flock. The former is the spirit of individualism, "business," and our law, the latter the spirit of socialism and science and—khaki.... They are both in all of us, they fluctuate from day to day; first one is ascendant and then the other.

War does not so much tilt the balance as accentuate the difference. One rich British landowner sneaks off to New York

State to set up a home there and evade taxation; another turns his mansion into a hospital and goes off to help Serbian refugees. Acts of baseness or generosity are contagious; this man will give himself altogether because of a story of devotion, this man declares he will do nothing until Sir F.E. Smith goes to the front. And the would-be prophet of what is going to happen must guess the relative force of these most impalpable and uncertain things.

This Braintree-Bocking boundary which runs down the middle of the road is to be found all over the world. You will find it in Ireland and the gentlemen who trade on the jealousies of the north side and the gentlemen who trade on the jealousies of the south. You will find it in England among the good people who would rather wreck the Empire than work honestly and fairly with Labour. There are not only parish boundaries, but park boundaries and class and sect boundaries. You will find the Bocking-Braintree line too at a dozen points on a small scale map of Europe.... These Braintree-Bocking lines are the barbed-wire entanglements between us and the peace of the world. Against these entanglements in every country the new spirit struggles in many thousands of minds. Where will it be strongest? Which country will get clear first, get most rapidly to work again, have least of the confusion and wrangling that must in some degree occur everywhere? Will any country go altogether to pieces in hopeless incurable discord?

Now I believe that the answer to that last question is "No." And my reason for that answer is the same as my reason for believing that the association of the Pledged Allies will not break up after the war; it is that I believe that this war is going to end not in the complete smashing up and subjugation of either side, but in a general exhaustion that will make the recrudescence of the war still possible but very terrifying.

Mars will sit like a giant above all human affairs for the next two decades, and the speech of Mars is blunt and plain. He will say to us all: "Get your houses in order. If you squabble among yourselves, waste time, litigate, muddle, snatch profits and shirk obligations, I will certainly come down upon you again. I have taken all your men between eighteen and fifty, and killed and maimed such as I pleased; millions of them. I have wasted your substance—contemptuously. Now, mark you, you have multitudes of male children between the ages of nine and nineteen running about among you. Delightful and beloved boys. And behind them come millions of delightful babies. Of these I have scarcely smashed and starved a paltry hundred thousand perhaps by the way. But go on muddling, each for himself and his parish and his family and none for all the world, go on in the old way, stick to-your 'rights,' stick to your 'claims' each one of you, make no concessions and no sacrifices, obstruct, waste, squabble, and presently I will come back again and take all that fresh harvest of life I have spared, all those millions that are now sweet children and dear little boys and youths, and I will squeeze it into red pulp between my hands, I will mix it with the mud of trenches and feast on it before your eyes, even more damnably than I have done with your grown-up sons and young men. And I have taken most of your superfluities already; next time I will take your barest necessities."

So the red god, Mars; and in these days of universal education the great mass of people will understand plainly now that that is his message and intention. Men who cannot be swayed by the love of order and creation may be swayed by the thought of death and destruction.... There, I think, is the overriding argument that will burst the proprietorships and divisions and boundaries, the web of ineffectiveness that has held the world so long. Labour returning from the trenches to its country and demanding promptness, planning, generous and devoted leaderships and organisation, demanding that the usurer and financier, the landlord and lawyer shall, if need be, get themselves altogether out of the way, will have behind its arguments the thought of the enemy still unsubdued, still formidable, recovering. Both sides will feel that. This world is a more illuminated world than 1816; a thousand questions between law and duty have been discussed since then; beyond

H. G. Wells

all comparison we know better what we are doing. I think the broad side of John Smith (and Sir John Smith and John Smith, K.C.) will get the better of his narrow ends—and that so it will be with Jean Dupont and Hans Meyer and the rest of them. There may be riots here and there; there may be some pretty considerable rows; but I do not think there is going to be a chaotic and merely destructive phase in Great Britain or any Western European country. I cast my guess for reconstruction and not for revolt.

V

HOW FAR WILL EUROPE GO
TOWARD SOCIALISM?

A number of people are saying that this war is to be the end of Individualism. "Go as you please" has had its death-blow. Out of this war, whatever else emerges, there will emerge a more highly organized State than existed before—that is to say, a less individualistic and more socialistic State. And there seems a heavy weight of probability on the side of this view. But there are also a number of less obvious countervailing considerations that may quite possibly modify or reverse this tendency.

In this chapter an attempt is to be made to strike a balance between the two systems of forces, and guess how much will be private and how much public in Europe in 1930, or thereabouts.

The prophets who foretell the coming of Socialism base their case on three sets of arguments. They point out, first, the failure of individual enterprise to produce a national efficiency comparable to the partial State Socialism of Germany, and the extraordinary, special dangers inherent in private property that the war has brought to light; secondly, to the scores of approaches to practical Socialism that have been forced upon Great Britain—for example, by the needs of the war; and, thirdly, to the obvious necessities that will confront the British Empire and the Allies generally after the war—necessities that no unorganised private effort can hope to meet effectively.

H. G. Wells

All these arguments involve the assumption that the general understanding of the common interest will be sufficient to override individual and class motives; an exceedingly doubtful assumption, to say the least of it. But the general understanding of the common interest is most likely to be kept alive by the sense of a common danger, and we have already arrived at the conclusion that Germany is going to be defeated but not destroyed in this war, and that she will be left with sufficient vitality and sufficient resentment and sufficient of her rancid cultivated nationalism to make not only the continuance of the Alliance after the war obviously advisable and highly probable, but also to preserve in the general mind for a generation or so that sense of a common danger which most effectually conduces to the sweeping aside of merely personal and wasteful claims. Into the consequences of this we have now to look a little more closely.

It was the weaknesses of Germany that made this war, and not her strength. The weaknesses of Germany are her Imperialism, her Junkerism, and her intense, sentimental Nationalism; for the former would have no German ascendancy that was not achieved by force, and, with the latter, made the idea of German ascendancy intolerable to all mankind. Better death, we said. And had Germany been no more than her Court, her Junkerism, her Nationalism, the whole system would have smashed beneath the contempt and indignation of the world within a year.

But the strength of Germany has saved her from that destruction. She was at once the most archaic and modern of states. She was Hohenzollern, claiming to be Caesar, and flaunting a flat black eagle borrowed from Imperial Rome; and also she was the most scientific and socialist of states. It is her science and her Socialism that have held and forced back the avengers of Belgium for more than a year and a half. If she has failed as a conqueror, she has succeeded as an organisation. Her ambition has been thwarted, and her method has been vindicated. She will, I think, be so far defeated in the contest of endurance which is now in progress that she will have to give up every scrap of territorial advantage she has gained; she may lose most of her Colonial Empire; she may be obliged to complete her modernisation by abandoning her militant Imperialism; but she will have at least the satisfaction of producing far profounder changes in the chief of her antagonists than those she herself will undergo.

The Germany of the Hohenzollerns had its mortal wound at the Marne; the Germany we fight to-day is the Germany of Krupp and Ostwald. It is merely as if she had put aside a mask that had blinded her. She was methodical and civilised except for her head and aim; she will become entirely methodical. But the Britain and Russia and France she fights are lands full of the spirit of undefined novelty. They are being made over far more completely. They are being made over, not in spite of the war, but because of the war. Only by being made over can they win the war. And if they do not win the war, then they are bound to be made over. They are not merely putting aside old things, but they are forming and organising within themselves new structures, new and more efficient relationships, that will last far beyond the still remote peace settlement.

What this war has brought home to the consciousness of every intelligent man outside the German system, with such thoroughness as whole generations of discussion and peace experience could never have achieved, is a double lesson: that Germany had already gone far to master when she blundered into the war; firstly, the waste and dangers of individualism, and, secondly, the imperative necessity of scientific method in public affairs. The waste and dangers of individualism have had a whole series of striking exemplifications both in Europe and America since the war began. Were there such a thing as a Socialist propaganda in existence, were the so-called socialistic organizations anything better than a shabby little back-door into contemporary politics, those demonstrations would be hammering at the mind of everyone. It may be interesting to recapitulate some of the most salient instances.

The best illustration, perhaps, of the waste that arises out of individualism is to be found in the extreme dislocation of the privately owned transit services of Great Britain at the present time. There is no essential reason whatever why food and fuel in Great Britain should be considerably dearer than they are under peace conditions. Just the same home areas are under cultivation, just the same foreign resources are available; indeed, more foreign supplies are available because we have intercepted those that under normal conditions would have gone to Germany. The submarine blockade of Britain is now a negligible factor in this question.

Despite these patent conditions there has been, and is, a steady increase in the cost of provisions, coal, and every sort of necessity. This increase means an increase in the cost of production of many commodities, and so contributes again to the general scarcity. This is the domestic aspect of a difficulty that has also its military side. It is not sufficient merely to make munitions; they must also be delivered, Great Britain is suffering very seriously from congestion of the railways. She suffers both in social and military efficiency, and she is so suffering because her railways, instead of being planned as one great and simple national distributing system, have grown up under conditions of clumsy, dividend-seeking competition.

Each great railway company and combination has worked its own areas, and made difficulties and aggressions at the boundaries of its sphere of influence; here are inconvenient junctions and here unnecessary duplications; nearly all the companies come into London, each taking up its own area of expensive land for goods yards, sidings, shunting grounds, and each regardless of any proper correlation with the other; great areas of the County of London are covered with their idle trucks and their separate coal stores; in many provincial towns you will find two or even three railway stations at opposite ends of the town; the streets are blocked by the vans and trolleys of the several companies tediously handing about goods that could be dealt with at a tenth of the cost in time and labour at a central clearing-house, did such a thing exist; and each system has its vast separate staff, unaccustomed to work with any other staff.

Since the war began the Government has taken over the general direction of this disarticulated machinery, but no one with eyes who travels about England now can fail to remark, in the miles and miles of waiting loaded trucks on every siding, the evidences of mischievous and now almost insuperable congestion. The trucks of each system that have travelled on to another still go back, for the most part, *empty* to their own; and thousands of privately owned trucks, which carry cargo only one way, block our sidings. Great Britain wastes men and time to a disastrous extent in these needless shuntings and handlings.

Here, touching every life in the community, is one instance of the muddle that arises naturally out of the individualistic method of letting public services grow up anyhow without a plan, or without any direction at all except the research for private profit.

A second series of deficiencies that the war has brought to light in the too individualistic British State is the entire want of connection between private profit and public welfare. So far as the interests of the capitalist go it does not matter whether he invests his money at home or abroad; it does not matter whether his goods are manufactured in London or Timbuctoo.

But what of the result? At the outbreak of the war Great Britain found that a score of necessary industries had drifted out of the country, because it did not "pay" any private person to keep them here. The shortage of dyes has been amply discussed as a typical case. A much graver one that we may now write about was the shortage of zinc. Within a month or so of the outbreak of the war the British Government had to take urgent and energetic steps to secure this essential ingredient of cartridge cases. Individualism had let zinc refining drift to Belgium and Germany; it was the luck rather than the merit of Great Britain that one or two refineries still existed.

H. G. Wells

Still more extraordinary things came to light in the matter of the metal supply. Under an individualistic system you may sell to the highest bidder, and anyone with money from anywhere may come in and buy. Great supplies of colonial ores were found to be cornered by semi-national German syndicates. Supplies were held up by these contracts against the necessities of the Empire. And this was but one instance of many which have shown that, while industrial development in the Allied countries is still largely a squabbling confusion of little short-sighted, unscientific, private profit-seeking owners, in Germany it has been for some years increasingly run on far-seeing collectivist lines. Against the comparatively little and mutually jealous British or American capitalists and million-aires Germany pits itself as a single great capitalist and competitor. She has worked everywhere upon a comprehensive plan. Against her great national electric combination, for example, only another national combination could stand. As it was, Germany—in the way of business—wired and lit (and examined) the forts at Liege. She bought and prepared a hundred strategic centres in individualistic Belgium and France.

So we pass from the fact that individualism is hopeless muddle to the fact that the individualist idea is one of limitless venality, Who can buy, may control. And Germany, in her long scheming against her individualist rivals, has not simply set herself to buy and hold the keys and axles of their economic machinery. She has set herself, it must be admitted, with a certain crudity and little success, but with unexampled vigour, to buy the minds of her adversaries. The Western nations have taken a peculiar pride in having a free Press; that is to say, a Press that may be bought by anyone. Our Press is constantly bought and sold, in gross and detail, by financiers, advertisers, political parties, and the like. Germany came into the market rather noisily, and great papers do to a large extent live in glass houses; but her efforts have been sufficient to exercise the minds of great numbers of men with the problem of what might have happened in the way of national confusion if the German attack had been more subtly conceived....

It is only a partial answer to this difficulty to say that a country that is so nationalist and aggressive as Germany is incapable of subtle conceptions. The fact remains that in Great Britain at the present time there are newspaper proprietors who would be good bargains for Germany at two million pounds a head, and that there was no effectual guarantee in the individualistic system, but only our good luck and the natural patriotism of the individuals concerned that she did not pick up these bargains before trading with the enemy became illegal. It happened, for example, that Lord Northcliffe was public-spirited, That was the good luck of Great Britain rather than her merit. There was nothing in the individualistic system to prevent Germany from buying up the entire Harmsworth Press—*The Times, Daily Mail*, and all—five years before the war, and using it to confuse the national mind, destroy the national unity, sacrifice the national interests, and frustrate the national will.

Not only the newspapers, but the news-agents and booksellers of both Great Britain and America are entirely at the disposal of any hostile power which chooses to buy them up quietly and systematically. It is merely a question of wealth and cleverness. And if the failure of the Germans to grip the Press of the French and English speaking countries has been conspicuous, she has been by no means so unsuccessful in—for example—Spain. At the present time the thought and feeling of the Spanish speaking world is being *educated* against the Allies. The Spanish mind has been sold by its custodians into German control.

Muddle and venality do not, however, exhaust the demonstrated vices of individualism. Individualism encourages desertion and treason. Individualism permits base private people to abscond with the national resources and squeeze a profit out of national suffering. In the early stages of the war some bright minds conceived the idea of a corner in drugs. It is not illegal; it is quite the sort of thing that appeals to the individualistic frame of mind as entirely meritorious. As the *New Statesman* put it recently: "The happy owners of the world's available stock of a few indispensable drugs did not refrain from making, not only the various Governments, but also all the sick people of the world pay double, and even tenfold, prices for what was essential to relieve pain and save life. What fortunes were thus made we shall probably never know, any more than we shall know the tale of the men and women and children who suffered and died because of their inability to pay, not the cost of production of what would have saved them, but the unnecessarily enhanced price that the chances of the market enabled the owners to exact."

And another bright instance of the value of individualism is the selling of British shipping to neutral buyers just when the country is in the most urgent need of every ship it can get, and the deliberate transfer to America of a number of British businesses to evade paying a proper share of the national bill in taxation. The English who have gone to America at different times have been of very different qualities; at the head of the list are the English who went over in the *Mayflower*; at the bottom will be the rich accessions of this war....

And perhaps a still more impressive testimony to the rottenness of these "business men," upon whom certain eccentric voices call so amazingly to come and govern us, is the incurable distrust they have sown in the minds of labour. Never was an atmosphere of discipline more lamentable than that which has grown up in the factories, workshops, and great privately owned public services of America and Western Europe. The men, it is evident, *expect* to be robbed and cheated at every turn. I can only explain their state of mind by supposing that they have been robbed and cheated. Their scorn and contempt for their employees' good faith is limitless. Their *morale* is undermined by an invincible distrust.

It is no good for Mr. Lloyd George to attempt to cure the gathered ill of a century with half an hour or so of eloquence. When Great Britain, in her supreme need, turns to the workmen she has trained in the ways of individualism for a century, she reaps the harvest individualism has sown. She has to fight with that handicap. Every regulation for the rapid mobilisation of labour is scrutinised to find the trick in it.

And they find the trick in it as often as not. Smart individualistic "business experience" has been at the draughtsman's elbow. A man in an individualistic system does not escape from class ideas and prejudices by becoming an official. There is profound and bitter wisdom in the deep distrust felt by British labour for both military and industrial conscription.

The breakdown of individualism has been so complete in Great Britain that we are confronted with the spectacle of this great and ancient kingdom reconstructing itself perforce, while it wages the greatest war in history. A temporary nationalisation of land transit has been improvised, and only the vast, deep-rooted, political influence of the shipowners and coalowners have staved off the manifestly necessary step of nationalising shipping and coal. I doubt if they will be able to stave it off to the end of the long struggle which is still before us if the militarism of Germany is really to be arrested and discredited. Expropriation and not conscription will be the supreme test of Britain's loyalty to her Allies.

The British shipowners, in particular, are reaping enormous but precarious profits from the war. The blockade of Britain, by the British shipowners is scarcely less effective than the blockade of Germany by Britain. With an urgent need of every ship for the national supplies, British ships, at the present moment of writing this, are still carrying cheap American automobiles to Australia. They would carry munitions to Germany if their owners thought they had a sporting chance of not getting caught at it. These British shipowners are a pampered class with great political and social influence, and no doubt as soon as the accumulating strain of the struggle tells to the extent of any serious restriction of their advantage and prospects, we shall see them shifting to the side of the at present negligible group of British pacifists. I do not think one can count on any limit to their selfishness and treason.

I believe that the calculations of some of these extreme and apparently quite unreasonable "pacifists" are right. Before the war is over there will be a lot of money in the pacifist business. The rich curs of the West End will join hands with the labour curs of the Clyde. The base are to be found in all classes, but I doubt if they dominate any. I do not believe that any interest or group of interests in Great Britain can stand in the way of the will of the whole people to bring this struggle to a triumphant finish at any cost. I do not believe that the most sacred ties of personal friendship and blood relationship with influential people can save either shipowners or coalowners or army contractors to the end.

There will be no end until these profit-makings are arrested. The necessary "conscriptions of property" must come about in Great Britain because there is no alternative but failure in the war, and the British people will not stand failure. I believe that the end of the war will see, not only transit, but shipping, collieries, and large portions of the machinery of food and drink production and distribution no longer under the administration of private ownership, but under a sort of provisional public administration. And very many British factories will be in the same case.

Two years ago no one would have dared to prophesy the tremendous rearrangement of manufacturing machinery which is in progress in Britain to-day. Thousands of firms of engineers and manufacturers of all sorts, which were flourishing in 1914, exist to-day only as names, as shapes, as empty shells. Their staffs have been shattered, scattered, reconstructed; their buildings enlarged and modified; their machinery exchanged, reconstituted, or taken. The reality is a vast interdependent national factory that would have seemed incredible to Fourier.

It will be as impossible to put back British industrialism into the factories and forms of the pre-war era as it would be to restore the Carthaginian Empire. There is a new economic Great Britain to-day, emergency made, jerry-built no doubt, a gawky, weedy giant, but a giant who may fill out to such dimensions as the German national system has never attained. Behind it is an *idea*, a new idea, the idea of the nation as one great economic system working together, an idea which could not possibly have got into the sluggish and conservative British intelligence in half a century by any other means than the stark necessities of this war.... Great Britain cannot retrace those steps even if she would, and so she will be forced to carry this process of reconstruction through. And what is happening to Great Britain must, with its national differences, be happening to France and Russia. Not only for war ends, but for peace ends, behind the front and sustaining the front, individualities are being hammered together into common and concerted activities.

At the end of this war Great Britain will find herself with this great national factory, this great national organisation of labour, planned, indeed, primarily to make war material, but convertible with the utmost ease to the purposes of automobile manufacture, to transit reconstruction, to electrical enginee-ring, and endless such uses.

France and Russia will be in a parallel case. All the world will be exhausted, and none of the Allies will have much money to import automobiles, railway material, electrical gear, and so on, from abroad. Moreover, it will be a matter of imperative necessity for them to get ahead of the Central Powers with their productive activities. We shall all be too poor to import from America, and we shall be insane to import from Germany. America will be the continent with the long purse, prepared to buy rather than sell. Each country will have great masses of soldiers waiting to return to industrial life, and will therefore be extremely indisposed to break up any existing productive organisation.

In the face of these facts, will any of the Allied Powers be so foolish as to disband this great system of national factories and nationally worked communications? Moreover, we have already risked the prophecy that this war will not end with

H. G. Wells

such conclusiveness as to justify an immediate beating out of our swords into ploughshares. There will be a military as well as a social reason for keeping the national factories in a going state.

What more obvious course, then, than to keep them going by turning them on to manufacture goods of urgent public necessity? There are a number of modern commodities now practically standardised: the bicycle, the cheap watch, the ordinary tradesman's delivery automobile, the farmer's runabout, the country doctor's car, much electric-lighting material, dynamos, and so forth. And also, in a parallel case, there is shipbuilding. The chemical side of munition work can turn itself with no extreme difficulty to the making of such products as dyes.

We face the fact, then, that either the State must go on with this production, as it can do, straight off from the signing of peace, converting with a minimum of friction, taking on its soldiers as they are discharged from the army as employees with a minimum waste of time and a minimum of social disorder, and a maximum advantage in the resumption of foreign trade, or there will be a dangerous break-up of the national factory system, a time of extreme chaos and bitter unemployment until capital accumulates for new developments. The risks of social convulsion will be enormous. And there is small hope that the Central Powers, and particularly industrial Germany, will have the politeness to wait through the ten or twelve years of economic embarrassment that a refusal to take this bold but obviously advantageous step into scientific Socialism will entail.

But the prophet must be on his guard against supposing that, because a thing is highly desirable, it must necessarily happen; or that, because it is highly dangerous, it will be avoided. This bold and successful economic reconstruction upon national lines is not inevitable merely because every sound reason points us in that direction. A man may be very ill, a certain drug may be clearly indicated as the only possible remedy, but it does not follow that the drug is available, that the doctor will have the sense to prescribe it, or the patient the means to procure it or the intelligence to swallow it.

The experience of history is that nations do not take the obviously right course, but the obviously wrong one. The present prophet knows only his England, but, so far as England is concerned, he can cover a sheet of paper with scarcely a pause, jotting down memoranda of numberless forces that make against any such rational reconstruction. Most of these forces, in greater or less proportion, must be present in the case of every other country under consideration.

The darkest shadow upon the outlook of European civilisation at the present time is not the war; it is the failure of any co-operative spirit between labour and the directing classes. The educated and leisured classes have been rotten with indiv-idualism for a century; they have destroyed the confidence of the worker in any leadership whatever. Labour stands apart, intractable. If there is to be any such rapid conversion of the economic machinery as the opportunities and necessities of this great time demand, then labour must be taken into the confidence of those who would carry it through. It must be reassured and enlightened. Labour must know clearly what is being done; it must be an assenting co-operator. The stride to economic national service and Socialism is a stride that labour should be more eager to take than any other section of the community.

The first step in reassuring labour must be to bring the greedy private owner and the speculator under a far more drastic discipline than at present. The property-owning class is continually accusing labour of being ignorant, suspicious, and difficult; it is blind to the fact that it is itself profit-seeking by habit, greedy, conceited, and half educated.

Every step in the mobilisation of Great Britain's vast resources for the purposes of the war has been hampered by the tricks, the failures to understand, and the almost instinctive disloyallties of private owners. The raising of rents in Glasgow drove the infuriated workmen of the Clyde district into an unwilling strike. It was an exasperating piece of private selfishness, quite typical of the individualistic state of mind, and the failure to anticipate or arrest it on the part of the Government was a worse failure than Suvla Bay. And everywhere the officials of the Ministry of Munitions find private employers holding back workers and machinery from munition works, intriguing—more particularly through the Board of Trade—to have all sorts of manufactures for private profit recognised as munition work, or if that contention is too utterly absurd, then as work vitally necessary to the maintenance of British export trade and the financial position of the country. It is an undeniable fact that employers and men alike have been found far readier to risk their lives for their country than to lay aside any scale of profits to which they have grown accustomed.

This conflict of individualistic enterprise and class suspicion against the synthesis of the public welfare is not peculiar to Great Britain; it is probably going on with local variations in Germany, Russia, Italy, France, and, indeed, in every combatant country. Because of the individualistic forces and feelings, none of us, either friends or enemies, are really getting anything like our full possible result out of our national efforts. But in Germany there is a greater tradition of subordination; in France there is a greater clarity of mind than in any other country.

Great Britain and Russia in this, as in so many other matters, are at once close kindred and sharp antithesis. Each is mentally crippled by the corruption of its educational system by an official religious orthodoxy, and hampered by a Court which disowns any function of intellectual stimulus. Neither possesses a scientifically educated *class* to which it can look for the powerful handling of this great occasion; and each has acquired under these disadvantages the same strange faculty for producing sane resultants out of illogical confusions. It is the way of these unmethodical Powers to produce unexpected, vaguely formulated, and yet effective cerebral action—apparently from their backbones.

As I sit playing at prophecy, and turn over the multitudinous impressions of the last year in my mind, weighing the great necessities of the time against obstacles and petty-mindedness, I become more and more conscious of a third factor that is neither need nor obstruction, and that is the will to get things right that has been liberated by the war.

The new spirit is still but poorly expressed, but it will find expression. The war goes on, and we discuss this question of economic reconstruction as though it was an issue that lay between the labour that has stayed behind and the business men, for the most part old men with old habits of mind, who have stayed behind.

The real life of Europe's future lies on neither side of that opposition. The real life is mutely busy at present, saying little because of the uproar of the guns, and not so much learning as casting habits and shedding delusions. In the trenches there are workers who have broken with the old slacking and sabotage, and there are prospective leaders who have forgotten profit. The men between eighteen and forty are far too busy in the blood and mud to make much showing now, but to-morrow these men will be the nation.

When that third factor of the problem is brought in the outlook of the horoscope improves. The spirit of the war may be counted upon to balance and prevail against this spirit of individualism, this spirit of suspicion and disloyalty, which I fear more than anything else in the world.

I believe in the young France, young England, and young Russia this war is making, and so I believe that every European country will struggle along the path that this war has opened to a far more completely organised State than has existed ever before. The Allies will become State firms, as Germany was, indeed, already becoming before the war; setting private profit

H. G. Wells

aside in the common interest, handling agriculture, transport, shipping, coal, the supply of metals, the manufacture of a thousand staple articles, as national concerns.

In the face of the manifest determination of the Central Powers to do as much, the Allies will be forced also to link their various State firms together into a great allied trust, trading with a common interest and a common plan with Germany and America and the rest of the world.... Youth and necessity will carry this against selfishness, against the unimaginative, against the unteachable, the suspicious, the "*old fool.*"

But I do not venture to prophesy that this will come about as if it were a slick and easy deduction from present circumstances. Even in France I do not think things will move as lucidly and generously as that. There will be a conflict everywhere between wisdom and cunning, between the eyes of youth and the purblind, between energy and obstinacy.

The reorganisation of the European States will come about clumsily and ungraciously. At every point the sticker will be found sticking tight, holding out to be bought off, holding out for a rent or a dividend or a share, holding out by mere instinct. At every turn, too, the bawler will be loud and active, bawling suspicions, bawling accusations, bawling panic, or just simply bawling. Tricks, peculation, obstinacies, vanities—after this war men will still be men. But I do believe that through all the dust and din, the great reasons in the case, the steady constructive forces of the situation, will carry us.

I believe that out of the ruins of the nineteenth century system of private capitalism that this war has smashed for ever, there will arise, there does even now arise, in this strange scaffolding of national munition factories and hastily nationalised public services, the framework of a new economic and social order based upon national ownership and service.

Let us now recapitulate a little and see how far we have got in constructing a picture of the European community as it will be in fifteen or twenty years' time. Nominally it will be little more of a Socialist State than it is to-day, but, as a matter of fact, the ships, the railways, the coal and metal supply, the great metal industries, much engineering, and most agriculture, will be more or less completely under collective ownership, and certainly very completely under collective control. This does not mean that there will have been any disappearance of private property, but only that there will have been a very considerable change in its character; the owner will be less of controller but more of a creditor; he will be a *rentier* or an annuitant.

The burthen of this class upon the community will not be relatively quite so heavy as it would otherwise have been, because of a very considerable rise in wages and prices.

In a community in which all the great initiatives have been assumed by the State, the importance of financiers and promoters will have diminished relatively to the importance of administrative officials; the opportunities of private exploitation, indeed, will have so diminished that there will probably be far less evidence of great concentrations of private wealth in the European social landscape than there was before the war.

On the other hand, there will be an enormously increased *rentier* class drawing the interest of the war loans from the community, and maintaining a generally high standard of comfort. There will have been a great demand for administrative and technical abilities and a great stimulation of scientific and technical education. By 1926 we shall be going about a world that will have recovered very largely from the impoverishment of the struggle; we shall tour in State-manufactured automobiles upon excellent roads, and we shall live in houses equipped with a national factory electric light installation, and at every turn we shall be using and consuming the products of nationalized industry—and paying off the National Debt simultaneously, and reducing our burden of *rentiers*.

At the same time our boys will be studying science in their schools more thoroughly than they do now, and they will in many cases be learning Russian instead of Greek or German. More of our boys will be going into the public service, and fewer thinking of private business, and they will be going into the public service, not as clerks, but as engineers, technical chemists, manufacturers, State agriculturists, and the like. The public service will be less a service of clerks and more a service of practical men. The ties that bind France and Great Britain at the present moment will have been drawn very much closer. France, Belgium and England will be drifting towards a French-English bi-lingualism....

So much of our picture we may splash in now. Much that is quite essential remains to be discussed. So far we have said scarcely a word about the prospects of party politics and the problems of government that arise as the State ceases to be a mere impartial adjudicator between private individuals, and takes upon itself more and more of the direction of the general life of the community.

VI

LAWYER AND PRESS

The riddle of administration is the most subtle of all those that the would-be prophet of the things that are coming must attempt. We see the great modern States confronted now by vast and urgent necessities, by opportunities that may never recur. Individualism has achieved its inevitable failure; "go as you please" in a world that also contained aggressive militarism, has broken down. We live in a world of improvised State factories, commandeered railways, substituted labour and emergency arrangements. Our vague-minded, lax, modern democracy has to pull itself together, has to take over and administer and succeed with a great system of collective functions, has to express its collective will in some better terms than "go as you please," or fail.

And we find the affairs of nearly every great democratic State in the hands of a class of men not specially adapted to any such constructive or administrative work.

I am writing here now chiefly of the Western Allies. Russia is peculiar in having her administrative machine much more highly developed in relation to her general national life than the free democratic countries. She has to make a bureaucracy that has not hitherto been an example for efficiency into a bureaucracy that will be constructive, responsive, liberal, scientific, and efficient; the Western countries have to do the same with that oligarchy of politicians which, as Professor

H. G. Wells

Michels has recently pointed out in his striking book on "Political Parties," is the necessary reality of democratic government. By different methods the Eastern and Western Powers have to attain a common end. Both bureaucracy and pseudo-democratic oligarchy have to accomplish an identical task, to cement the pacific alliance of the Pledged Allies and to socialise their common industrial and economic life, so as to make it invulnerable to foreign attack.

Now in Great Britain, which is the democracy that has been most under the close observation of the present prophet, there is at present a great outcry against the "politician," and more particularly against the "lawyer-politician." He is our embarrassment. In him we personify all our difficulties. Let us consider the charges against this individual. Let us ask, can we do without him? And let us further see what chances there may be of so altering, qualifying, or balancing him as to minimize the evil of his influence. To begin with, let us run over the essentials of the charge against him.

It is with a modest blush that the present prophet recapitulates these charges. So early as the year 1902 he was lifting up his voice, not exactly in the wilderness but at least in the Royal Institution, against the legal as compared with the creative or futurist type of mind. The legal mind, he insisted, looks necessarily to the past. It is dilatory because it has no sense of coming things, it is uninventive and wasteful, it does not create, it takes advantage. It is the type of mind least able, under any circumstances, to organise great businesses, to plan campaigns, to adventure or achieve. "Wait and see" crystallises its spirit. Its resistance is admirable, and it has no "go." Nevertheless there is a tendency for power to gravitate in all democratic countries to the lawyer.

In the British system the normal faults of the lawyer are enhanced, and his predominance intensified, by certain peculiarities of our system. In the first place, he belongs to a guild of exceptional power. In Britain it happens that the unfortunate course was taken ages ago of bribing the whole legal profession to be honest. The British judges and law officers are stupendously overpaid in order to make them incorruptible; it is a poor but perhaps a well-merited compliment to their professional code. We have squared the whole profession to be individually unbribable.

The judges, moreover, in the Anglo-Saxon communities are appointed from among the leading barristers, an arrangement that a child can see is demoralising and inadvisable. And in Great Britain all the greatest salaries in the government service are reserved for the legal profession. The greatest prizes, therefore, before an energetic young man who has to make his way in Great Britain are the legal prizes, and his line of advancement to these lies, for all the best years of his life, not through the public service, but through the private practice of advocacy. The higher education, such as it is, in Great Britain, produces under the stimulus of these conditions an advocate as its finest flower. To go from the posing and chatter of the Union Debating Society to a university laboratory is, in Britain, to renounce ambition. Few men of exceptional energy will do that.

The national consequences of this state of affairs have been only too manifest throughout the conduct of the war. The British Government has developed all the strength and all the weakness of the great profession it represents. It has been uninventive, dilatory, and without initiative; it has been wasteful and evasive; but it has not been wanting in a certain eloquence and dignity, it has been wary and shrewd, and it has held on to office with the concentrated skill and determination of a sucker-fish. And the British mind, with a concentration and intensity unprecedented before the war, is speculating how it can contrive to get a different sort of ruler and administrator at work upon its affairs.

There is a disposition in the Press, and much of the private talk one hears, to get rid of lawyers from the control of national affairs altogether, to substitute "business men" or scientific men or "experts." That way lies dictatorship and Caesarism.

And even Great Britain is not so heedless of the experiences of other nations as to attempt again what has already been so abundantly worked out in national disaster across the Channel. The essential business of government is to deal between man and man; it is not to manage the national affairs in detail, but to secure the proper managers, investigators, administrators, generals, and so forth, to maintain their efficiency, and keep the balance between them. We cannot do without a special class of men for these interventions and controls. In other words, we cannot do without a special class of politicians. They may be elected by a public or appointed by an autocrat; at some point they have to come in. And this business of intervening between men and classes and departments in public life, and getting them to work together, is so closely akin to the proper work of a lawyer in dealing between men and men, that, unless the latter are absolutely barred from becoming the former, it is almost unavoidable that politicians should be drawn more abundantly from the lawyer class than from any other class in the community.

This is so much the case, that when the London *Times* turns in despair from a government of lawyers and looks about for an alternative, the first figure that presents itself is that distinguished advocate Sir Edward Carson!

But there is a difference between recognising that some sort of lawyer-politician is unavoidable and agreeing that the existing type of lawyer who is so largely accountable for the massive slowness, the confused action, the slovenliness rather than the weakness of purpose, shown by Great Britain in this war, is the only possible type, The British system of education and legal organisation is not the last word of human wisdom in these matters.

The real case we British have against our lawyers, if I may adopt an expressive colloquialism, is not that they are lawyers, but that they are such infernal lawyers. They trail into modern life most of the faults of a mediaeval guild. They seem to have no sense of the State they could develop, no sense of the future they might control. Their law and procedure has never been remodelled upon the framework of modern ideas; their minds are still set to the tune of mediaeval bickerings, traditionalism, and State blindness. They are mystery dealers, almost unanimously they have resisted giving the common man the protection of a code.

In the United Kingdom we have had no Napoleon to override the profession. It is extraordinary how complete has been their preservation of barbaric conceptions. Even the doctor is now largely emancipated from his archaic limitations as a skilled retainer. He thinks more and more of the public health, and less and less of his patron. The more recent a profession the less there is of the individualistic personal reference; scientific research, for example, disavows and forbids every personal reference.

But while everyone would be shocked at some great doctor, or some great research institution, in these days of urgent necessity spending two or three weeks on the minor ailments of some rich person's lapdog, nobody is scandalised at the spectacle of Sir Edward Carson and a costly law court spending long days upon the sordid disputes that centre upon young Master Slingsby's ear—whether it is the Slingsby family ear or the ear of a supposititious child—a question that any three old women might be trusted to settle. After that he rests for a fortnight and recuperates, and returns—to take up a will case turning upon the toy rabbits and suchlike trifles which entertained the declining years of a nonagenarian. This, when we are assured that the country awaits Sir Edward as its Deliverer. It is as if Lord Kitchener took a month off to act at specially high rates for the "movies." Our standard for the lawyer is older and lower than it is for other men.

There is no more reason nowadays why a lawyer should look to advocacy as a proper use of his knowledge than that a doctor should make private poisoning the lucrative side of his profession. There is no reason why a court of law should ignore the plain right of the commonweal to intervene in every case between man and man. There is every reason why trivial disputes about wills and legitimacy should not be wasting our national resources at the present time, when nearly every other form of waste is being restrained. The sound case against the legal profession in Anglo-Saxon countries is not that it is unnecessary, but that it is almost incredibly antiquated, almost incredibly careless of the public well-being, and that it corrupts or dwarfs all the men who enter it.

Our urgent need is not so much to get rid of the lawyer from our affairs as to get rid of the wig and gown spirit and of the special pleader, and to find and develop the new lawyer, the lawyer who is not an advocate, who is not afraid of a code, who has had some scientific education, and whose imagination has been quickened by the realisation of life as creative opportunity. We want to emancipate this profession from its ancient guild restrictions—the most anti-social and disastrous of all such restrictions—to destroy its disgraceful traditions of over-payment and fee-snatching, to insist upon a scientific philosophical training for its practitioners, to make the practice of advocacy a fall from grace, and to bar professional advocates from the bench.

In the British trenches now there must be many hundreds of fine young lawyers, still but little corrupted, who would be only too glad to exchange the sordid vulgarities and essential dishonour of a successful lawyer's career under the old conditions for lives of service and statecraft....

No observer of the general trend of events in Europe will get any real grasp of what is happening until he realises the cardinal importance of the reactions that centre upon this question. The current development of political institutions and the possible development of a new spirit and method in the legal profession are so intimately interwoven as to be practically one and the same question. The international question is, can we get a new Germany? The national question everywhere is, can we get a better politician?

The widely prevalent discontent with the part played by the lawyer in the affairs of all the Western Allies is certain to develop into a vigorous agitation for legal reconstruction. In the case of every other great trade union the war has exacted profound and vital concessions. The British working men, for example, have abandoned scores of protective restrictions upon women's labour, upon unskilled labour, for which they have fought for generations; they have submitted to a virtual serfdom that the nation's needs might be supplied; the medical profession has sent almost too large a proportion of its members to the front; the scientific men, the writers, have been begging to be used in any capacity at any price or none; the Ministry of Munitions is full of unpaid workers, and so on.

The British legal profession and trade union alone has made no sign of any disposition to relax its elaborate restrictions upon the labour of amateurs and women, or to abate one jot or one tittle of its habitual rewards. There has been no attempt to reduce the costly law officers of the Government, for example, or to call in the help of older men or women to release law officers who are of military experience or age.

And I must admit that there are small signs of the advent of the "new lawyer," at whose possibility I have just flung a hopeful glance, to replace the existing mass of mediaeval unsoundness. Barristers seem to age prematurely—at least in Great Britain—unless they are born old. In the legal profession one hears nothing of "the young"; one hears only of "smart juniors." Reform and progressive criticism in the legal profession, unlike all other professions, seem to be the monopoly of the retired.

Nevertheless, Great Britain is as yet only beginning to feel the real stresses of the war; she is coming into the full strain a year behind France, Germany, and Russia; and after the war there lies the possibility of still more violent stresses; so that what is as yet a mere cloud of criticism and resentment at our lawyer-politicians and privileged legal profession may gather to a great storm before 1918 or 1919.

I am inclined to foretell as one most highly probable development of the present vague but very considerable revolt against the lawyer in British public life, first, some clumsy proposals or even attempts to leave him out, and use "business men," soldiers, admirals, dictators, or men of science, in his place—which is rather like throwing away a blottesque fountain-pen and trying to write with a walking-stick or a revolver or a flash-light—and then when that is found to be impossible, a resolute attempt to clean and reconstitute the legal profession on modern and more honourable lines; a movement into which, quite possibly, a number of the younger British lawyers, so soon as they realise that the movement is good enough to risk careers upon, may throw themselves. A large share in such a reform movement, if it occurs, will be brought about by the Press; by which I mean not simply the periodical Press, but all books and contemporary discussion. It is only by the natural playing off of Press against lawyer-politician that democratic States can ever come to their own.

And that brings me to the second part of this question, which is whether, quite apart from the possible reform and spiritual rebirth of the legal profession, there is not also the possibility of balancing and correcting its influence. In ancient Hebrew history—it may be a warning rather than a precedent—there were two great forces, one formal, conservative and corrupting, the other undisciplined, creative, and destructive; the first was the priest, the second the prophet. Their interaction is being extraordinarily paralleled in the Anglo-Saxon democracies by the interaction of lawyer-politician and Press to-day.

If the lawyer-politician is unavoidable, the Press is indispensable. It is not in the clash and manoeuvres and mutual correction of party, but in the essential conflict of political authority on the one hand and Press on the other that the future of democratic government apparently lies. In the clearer, simpler case of France, a less wealthy and finer type of lawyer interacts with a less impersonal Press. It is in the great contrasts and the essential parallelism of the French and the

Anglo-Saxon democratic systems that one finds the best practical reason for anticipating very profound changes in these two inevitables of democracy, the Press and the lawyer-politician, and for assuming that the method of democracy has still a vast range of experimental adjustment between them still untried. Such experimental adjustment will be the chief necessity and business of political life in every country of the world for the next few decades.

The lawyer-politician and the Press are as it were the right and left hands of a modern democracy. The war has brought this out clearly. It has ruptured the long-weakened bonds that once linked this and that newspaper with this and that party. For years the Press of all the Western democracies has been drifting slowly away from the tradition—it lasted longest and was developed most completely in Great Britain—that-newspapers were party organs.

In the novels of Disraeli the Press appears as an ambiguously helpful person who is asked out to dinner, who is even admitted to week-end conferences, by the political great. He takes his orders from the Whig peers or the Tory peers. At his greatest he advises them respectfully. But that was in the closing days of the British oligarchy; that was before modern democracy had begun to produce its characteristic political forms. It is not so very much more than a century ago that Great Britain had her first lawyer Prime Minister. Through all the Napoleonic wars she was still a country ruled by great feudal landlords, and gentlemen adventurers associated with them. The lawyers only came to their own at the close of the great Victorian duet of Disraeli and Gladstone, the last of the political gentlemen adventurers. It is only now, in the jolts and dissatisfactions of this war, that Great Britain rubs her eyes and looks at her government as it is.

The old oligarchy established the tradition of her diplomacy. Illiberal at home, it was liberal abroad; Great Britain was the defender of nationality, of constitutionalism, and of the balance of power against the holy alliance. In the figure of such a gentleman as Sir Edward Grey the old order mingles with the new. But most of his colleagues are cf the new order. They would have been incredible in the days of Lord Melbourne. In its essential quality the present British Government is far more closely akin to the French than it is to its predecessor of a hundred years ago. Essentially it is a Government of lawyer-politicians with no close family ties or intimate political traditions and prejudices. And its natural and proper corrective is the Press, over which it fails to exercise now even a shadow of the political and social influence that once kept that power in subjection.

It is the way with all human institutions; they remain in appearance long after they have passed away in reality. It is on record that the Roman senate still thought Rome was a republic in the third century of the Christian era. It is nothing wonderful, therefore, that people suppose that the King, the Lords, and the Commons, debating through a Ministry and an Opposition, still govern the British Empire. As a matter of fact it is the lawyer-politicians, split by factions that simulate the ancient government and opposition, who rule, under a steadily growing pressure and checking by the Press. Since this war began the Press has released itself almost inadvertently from its last association with the dying conflicts of party politics, and has taken its place as a distinct power in the realm, claiming to be more representative of the people than their elected representatives, and more expressive of the national mind and will.

Now there is considerable validity in this claim. It is easy to say that a paper may be bought by any proprietor and set to put what he chooses into the public mind. As a matter of fact, buying a newspaper is far more costly and public a proceeding than buying a politician. And if on the one hand the public has no control over what is printed in a paper, it has on the other the very completest control over what is read. A politician is checked by votes cast once in several years, a newspaper is checked by sales that vary significantly from day to day. A newspaper with no circulation is a newspaper that does not matter; a few weeks will suffice to show if it has carried its public with it or gone out of influence. It is absurd to speak of a newspaper as being less responsible than a politician.

Nevertheless, the influence of a great newspaper is so much greater than that of any politician, and its power more particularly for mischief—for the creation of panic conditions, for example—so much swifter, that it is open to question whether the Press is at present sufficiently held to its enormous responsibilities.

Let us consider its weaknesses at the present time, let us ask what changes in its circumstances are desirable in the public interest, and what are likely to come about. We have already reckoned upon the Press as a chief factor in the adequate criticism, cleansing, and modernisation of the British lawyer-politician; is there any power to which we may look for the security of the Press? And I submit the answer is the Press. For while the legal profession is naturally homogeneous, the Press is by nature heterogeneous. Dog does not eat dog, nor lawyer, lawyer; but the newspapers are sharks and cannibals, they are in perpetual conflict, the Press is a profession as open as the law is closed; it has no anti-social guild feeling; it washes its dirty linen in public by choice and necessity, and disdains all professional etiquette. Few people know what criticisms of the Lord Chief Justice may have ripened in the minds of Lord Halsbury or Sir Edward Carson, but we all know, to a very considerable degree of accuracy, the worst of what this great journalist or group of newspaper proprietors thinks of that.

We have, therefore, considerable reason for regarding the Press as being, in contrast with the legal profession, a self-reforming body. In the last decade there has been an enormous mass of criticism of the Press by the Press. There has been a tendency to exaggerate its irresponsibility. A better case is to be made against it for what I will call, using the word in its least offensive sense, its venality. By venality I mean the fact, a legacy from the now happily vanishing age of individualism, that in theory and law at least anyone may own a newspaper

H. G. Wells

and sell it publicly or secretly to anyone, that its circulation and advertisement receipts may be kept secret or not as the proprietors choose, and that the proprietor is accountable to no one for any exceptional incomings or any sudden fluctuations in policy.

A few years ago we were all discussing who should buy *The Times*; I do not know what chances an agent of the Kaiser might not have had if he had been sufficiently discreet. This venality will be far more dangerous to the Allied countries after the war than during its continuance. So long as the state of war lasts there are prompt methods available for any direct newspaper treason, and it is in the neutral countries only that the buying and selling of papers against the national interest has occurred to any marked extent.

Directly peace is signed, unless we provide for the event beforehand, our Press will pass under neutral conditions. There will be nothing to prevent, for example, any foreseeing foreign power coming into Great Britain, offering to buy up not only this paper or that, but also, what is far more important, to buy up the great book and newspaper distributing firms. These vitally important public services, so far as law and theory go, will be as entirely in the market as railway tickets at a station unless we make some intelligent preventive provision. Unless we do, and if, as is highly probable, peace puts no immediate stop to international malignity, the Germans will be bigger fools than I think them if they do not try to get hold of these public services. It is a matter of primary importance in the outlook of every country in Europe, therefore, that it should insist upon and secure responsible native ownership of every newspaper and news and book distributing agency, and the most drastic punishment for newspaper corruption. Given that guarantee against foreign bribery, we may, I think, let free speech rage. This is so much a matter of common sense that I cannot imagine even British "wait and see" waiting for the inevitable assault upon our national journalistic virtue that will follow the peace.

So I spread out the considerations that I think justify our forecasting, in a very changed Great Britain and a changed Europe, firstly, a legal profession with a quickened conscience, a sense of public function and a reformed organisation, and, secondly, a Press, which is recognised and held accountable in law and in men's minds, as an estate of the realm, as something implicitly under oath to serve the State. I do not agree with Professor Michel's pessimistic conclusion that peace will bring back exacerbated party politics and a new era of futility to the democratic countries. I believe that the tremendous demonstration of this war (a demonstration that gains weight with every week of our lengthening effort), of the waste and inefficiency of the system of 1913-14, will break down at last even the conservatism of the most rigidly organised and powerful and out-of-date of all professions.

It is not only that I look to the indignation and energy of intelligent men who are outside our legal and political system to reform it, but to those who are in it now. A man may be quietly parasitic upon his mother, and yet incapable of matricide. So much of our national energy and ability has been attracted to the law in Great Britain that our nation, with our lawyers in modern clothing instead of wigs and gowns, lawyers who have studied science and social theory instead of the spoutings of Cicero and the loquacious artfulness of W.E. Gladstone, lawyers who look forward at the destiny of their country instead of backward and at the markings on their briefs, may yet astonish the world. The British lawyer really holds the future of the British Empire and, indeed, I could almost say, of the whole world in his hands at the present time, as much as any single sort of man can be said to hold it. Inside his skull imagination and a heavy devil of evil precedent fight for his soul and the welfare of the world. And generosity fights against tradition and individualism. Only the men of the Press have anything like the same great possibilities of betrayal.

To these two sorts of men the dim spirit of the nation looks for such leading as a democracy can follow. To them the men with every sort of special ability, the men of science, the men of this or that sort of administrative ability and experience, the men of creative gifts and habits, every sort of man who wants the world to get on, look for the removal (or the ingenious contrivance) of obstructions and entanglements, for the allaying (or the fomentation) of suspicion, misapprehension, and ignorant opposition, for administration (or class blackmail).

Yet while I sit as a prophetic amateur weighing these impalpable forces of will and imagination and habit and interest in lawyer, pressman, maker and administrator, and feeling by no means over-confident of the issue, it dawns upon me suddenly that there is another figure present, who has never been present before in the reckoning up of British affairs. It is a silent figure. This figure stands among the pressmen and among the lawyers and among the workers; for a couple of decades at least he will be everywhere in the British system; he is young and he is uniformed in khaki, and he brings with him a new spirit into British life, the spirit of the new soldier, the spirit of subordination to a common purpose....

France, which has lived so much farther and deeper and more bitterly than Britain, knows....[2]

[Footnote 2: In "An Englishman Looks at the World," a companion volume to the present one, which was first published by Messrs. Cassell early in 1914, and is now obtainable in a shilling edition, the reader will find a full discussion of the probable benefit of proportional representation in eliminating the party hack from political life. Proportional representation would probably break up party organizations altogether, and it would considerably enhance the importance and responsibility of the Press. It would do much to accelerate the development of the state of affairs here foreshadowed, in which the role of government and opposition under the party system will be played by elected representatives and Press respectively.]

VII

THE NEW EDUCATION

Some few months ago Mr. Harold Spender, in the *Daily News*, was calling attention to a very significant fact indeed. The higher education in England, and more particularly the educational process of Oxford and Cambridge, which has been going on continuously since the Middle Ages, is practically in a state of suspense. Oxford and Cambridge have stopped. They have stopped so completely that Mr. Spender can speculate whether they can ever pick up again and resume upon the old lines.

For my own part, as the father of two sons who are at present in mid-school, I hope with all my heart that they will not. I hope that the Oxford and Cambridge of unphilosophical classics and Little-go Greek for everybody, don's mathematics, bad French, ignorance of all Europe except Switzerland, forensic exercises in the Union Debating Society, and cant about the Gothic, the Oxford and Cambridge that turned boys full of life and hope and infinite possibility into barristers, politicians, mono-lingual diplomatists, bishops, schoolmasters, company directors, and remittance men, are even now dead.

Quite recently I passed through Cambridge, and, with the suggestions of Mr. Spender in my mind, I paused to savour the atmosphere of the place. He had very greatly understated the facts of the case. He laid stress upon the fact that instead of the normal four thousand undergraduates or so, there are now

H. G. Wells

scarcely four hundred. But before I was fairly in Cambridge I realised that that gives no idea of the real cessation of English education. Of the first seven undergraduates I saw upon the Trumpington road, one was black, three were coloured, and one of the remaining three was certainly not British, but, I should guess, Spanish-American. And it isn't only the undergraduates who have gone. All the dons of military age and quality have gone too, or are staying up not in caps and gowns, but in khaki; all the vigorous teachers are soldiering; there are no dons left except those who are unfit for service—and the clergy. Buildings, libraries, empty laboratories, empty lecture theatres, vestiges, refugees, neutrals, khaki; that is Cambridge to-day.

There never was before, there never may be again, so wonderful an opportunity for a cleaning-up and sweeping-out of those two places, and for a profitable new start in British education.

The cessation of Oxford and Cambridge does not give the full measure of the present occasion. All the other British universities are in a like case. And the schools which feed them have been practically swept clean of their senior boys. And not a tithe of any of this war class of schoolboys will ever go to the universities now, not a tithe of the war class of undergraduates will ever return. Between the new education and the old there will be a break of two school generations. For the next thirty or forty years an exceptional class of men will play a leading part in British affairs, men who will have learnt more from reality and less from lectures than either the generations that preceded or the generations that will follow them. The subalterns of the great war will form a distinct generation and mark an epoch. Their experiences of need, their sense of deficiencies, will certainly play a large part in the reconstitution of British education. *The stamp of the old system will not be on them.*

Now is the time to ask what sort of training should a university give to produce the ruling, directing, and leading men which it exists to produce? Upon that Great Britain will need to make up its mind speedily. It is not a matter for to-morrow or the day after; it is necessary to decide now what it is the Britain that is coming will need and want, and to set to work revising the admission and degree requirements, and reconstructing all those systems of public examinations for the public services that necessarily dominate school and university teaching, before the universities and schools reassemble. If the rotten old things once get together again, the rotten old things will have a new lease of life. This and no other is the hour for educational reconstruction. And it is in the decisions and readjustments of schools and lectures and courses, far more than anywhere else, that the real future of Great Britain will be decided. Equally true is this of all the belligerent countries. Much of the future has a kind of mechanical inevitableness, but here far more than anywhere else, can a few resolute and capable men mould the spirit and determine the quality of the Europe to come.

Now surely the chief things that are needed in the education of a ruling class are these—first, the selection and development of Character, then the selection and development of Capacity, and, thirdly, the imparting of Knowledge upon broad and comprehensive lines, and the power of rapidly taking up and using such detailed knowledge as may be needed for special occasions. It is upon the first count that the British schools and universities have been most open to criticism. We have found the British university-trained class under the fiery tests of this war an evasive, temporising class of people, individualistic, ungenerous, and unable either to produce or obey vigorous leadership. On the whole, it is a matter for congratulation, it says wonderful things for the inherent natural qualities of the English-speaking peoples, that things have proved no worse than they are, considering the nature of the higher education under which they have suffered.

Consider in what that educational process has consisted. Its backbone has been the teaching of Latin by men who can read, write, and speak it rather worse than a third-rate Babu speaks English, and of Ancient Greek by teachers who at best half know this fine lost language. They do not expect any real mastery of either tongue by their students, and naturally, therefore, no real mastery is ever attained. The boys and young men just muff about at it for three times as long as would be needed to master completely both those tongues if they had "live" teachers, and so they acquire habits of busy futility and petty pedantry in all intellectual processes that haunt them throughout life. There are also sterile mathematical studies that never get from "exercises" to practice. There is a pretence of studying philosophy based on Greek texts that few of the teachers and none of the taught can read comfortably, and a certain amount of history. The Modern History School at Oxford, for example, is the queerest collection of chunks of reading. English history from the beginning, with occasional glances at Continental affairs, European history for about a century, bits of economics, and—the *Politics* of Aristotle! It is not education; it is a jack-daw collection....This sort of jumble has been the essentials of the more pretentious type of "higher education" available in Great Britain up to the present.

In this manner, through all the most sensitive and receptive years of life, our boys have been trained in "how not to get there," in a variety of disconnected subjects, by men who have never "got there," and it would be difficult to imagine any curriculum more calculated to produce a miscellaneous incompetence. They have also, it happens, received a certain training in *savoir faire* through the collective necessities of school life, and a certain sharpening in the arts of advocacy through the debating society. Except for these latter helps, they have had to face the world with minds neither more braced, nor more trained, nor more informed than any "uneducated" man's.

Surely the first condition that should be laid down for the new education in Europe is that whatever is undertaken must be undertaken in grim earnest and done. It is ridiculous to talk about the "character-forming" value of any study that does not go through to an end. Manifestly Greek must be dropped as a part of the general curriculum for a highly educated man, for the simple reason that now there are scarcely any competent teachers, and because the sham of teaching it partially and pretentiously demoralises student and school alike. The claim of the clergy and so forth to "know" Greek is one of the many corrupting lies in British intellectual life. English comic writers never weary of sneering at the Hindu who claimed to be a "failed B.A.," but what is the ordinary classical degree man of an English university but a "failed" Greek scholar? Latin, too, must be either reduced to the position of a study supplementary to the native tongue, or brought up to an honest level of efficiency.

French and German in the case of the English, and English in the case of the French and Russians, are essentially governess languages; any intelligent boy or girl from a reasonably prosperous home ought to be able to read, write, and speak either before fifteen; they are to be taken by the way rather than regarded as a fundamental part of education. The French, German, or English literature and literary development up to and including contemporary work is, of course, an entirely different matter. But there can be no doubt of the great educational value of some highly inflected and well-developed language *taught by men to whom it is a genuine means of expression.* Educational needs and public necessity point alike to such languages as Russian or, in the case of Great Britain, Hindustani to supply this sound training.

If Great Britain means business after this war, if she is to do her duty by the Eastern world she controls, she will not stick at the petty expense of getting a few hundreds of good Russian and Hindu teachers into the country, and she will place Russian and Hindustani upon at least an equal footing with Greek in all her university and competitive examinations. Moreover, it is necessary to set a definite aim of application before university mathematical teaching. As the first condition of character-building in all these things, the student should do what he ostensibly sets out to do. No degree and no position should be attainable by half accomplishment.

Of course, languages and mathematics do not by any means

round off the education of a man of the leading classes. There is no doubt much exercise in their attainment, much value in their possession. But the essence of the higher education is now, as it always has been, philosophy; not the antiquated pretence of "reading" Plato and Aristotle, but the thorough and subtle examination of those great questions of life that most exercise and strengthen the mind. Surely that is the essential difference of the "educated" and the "common" man. The former has thought, and thought out thoroughly and clearly, the relations of his mind to the universe as a whole, and of himself to the State and life. A mind untrained in swift and adequate criticism is essentially an uneducated mind, though it has as many languages as a courier and as much computation as a bookie.

And what is our fundamental purpose in all this reform of our higher education? It is neither knowledge nor technical skill, but to make our young men talk less and think more, and to think more swiftly, surely, and exactly. For that we want less debating society and more philosophy, fewer prizes for forensic ability and more for strength and vigour of analysis. The central seat of character is the mind. A man of weak character thinks vaguely, a man of clear intellectual decisions acts with precision and is free from vacillation. A country of educated men acts coherently, smites swiftly, plans ahead; a country of confused education is a country of essential muddle.

It is as the third factor in education that the handling and experience of knowledge comes, and of all knowledge that which is most accessible, most capable of being handled with the greatest variety of educational benefit, so as to include the criticism of evidence, the massing of facts, the extraction and testing of generalisations, lies in the two groups of the biological sciences and the exact sciences. No doubt a well-planned system of education will permit of much varied specialisation, will, indeed, specialise those who have special gifts from a very early age, will have corners for Greek, Hebrew, Sanscrit, philology, archaeology, Christian theology, and so on, and so on; nevertheless, for that great mass of sound men of indeterminate all-round ability who are the intellectual and moral backbone of a nation, it is in scientific studies that their best training lies, studies most convenient to undertake and most readily applied in life. From either of the two groups of the sciences one may pass on to research or to technical applications leading directly to the public service. The biological sciences broaden out through psychology and sociology to the theory and practice of law, and to political life. They lead also to medical and agricultural administration. The exact sciences lead to the administrative work of industrialism, and to general economics.

These are the broad, clear lines of the educational necessities of a modern community, plain enough to see, so that every man who is not blinded by prejudice and self-interest can see them to-day. We have now before us a phase of opportunity in educational organisation that will never recur again. Now that the apostolic succession of the old pedagogy is broken, and the entire system discredited, it seems incredible that it can ever again be reconstituted in its old seats upon the old lines. In these raw, harsh days of boundless opportunity, the opportunity of the new education, because it is the most fundamental, is assuredly the greatest of all.

VIII

WHAT THE WAR IS DOING FOR WOMEN

Section 1

To discuss the effect of this war upon the relations of men and women to each other is to enter upon the analysis of a secular process compared with which even the vast convulsions and destructions of this world catastrophe appear only as jolts and incidents and temporary interruptions. There are certain matters that sustain a perennial development, that are on a scale beyond the dramatic happenings of history; wars, the movements of peoples and races, economic changes, such things may accelerate or stimulate or confuse or delay, but they cannot arrest the endless thinking out, the growth and perfecting of ideas, upon the fundamental relationships of human Beings. First among such eternally progressive issues is religion, the relationship of man to God; next in importance and still more immediate is the matter of men's relations to women. In such matters each phase is a new phase; whatever happens, there is no going back and beginning over again. The social life, like the religious life, must grow and change until the human story is at an end.

So that this war involves, in this as in so many matters, no fundamental set-back, no reversals nor restorations. At the most it will but realize things already imagined, release things latent. The nineteenth century was a period of unprecedented modification of social relationships; but great as these changes were, they were trivial in comparison with the changes in religious thought and the criticism of moral ideals. Hell was the basis of religious thinking in A.D. 1800, and the hangman was at the back of the law; in 1900 both Hell and the hangman seemed on the verge of extinction. The creative impulse was everywhere replacing fear and compulsion in human motives. The opening decade of the twentieth century was a period of unprecedented abundance in everything necessary to human life, of vast accumulated resources, of leisure and release. It was also, because of that and because of the changed social and religious spirit, a period of great social disorganisation and confused impulses.

We British can already look back to the opening half of 1914 as to an age gone for ever. Except that we were all alive then and can remember, it has become now almost as remote, almost as "historical," as the days before the French Revolution. Our days, our methods and reactions, are already so different. The greater part of the freedom of movement, the travel and going to and fro, the leisure, the plenty and carelessness, that distinguished early twentieth century life from early nineteenth century life, has disappeared. Most men are under military discipline, and every household economises. The whole British people has been brought up against such elementary realities of need, danger, and restraint as it never realised before. We discover that we had been living like Olympians in regard to worldly affairs, we had been irresponsibles, amateurs. Much of that fatness of life, the wrappings and trimmings of our life, has been stripped off altogether. That has not altered the bones of life; it has only made them plainer; but it has astonished us as much as if looking into a looking-glass one suddenly found oneself a skeleton. Or a diagram.

What was going on before this war in the relations of men and women is going on still, with more rapidity perhaps, and certainly with more thoroughness. The war is accentuating, developing, defining. Previously our discussions and poses and movements had merely the air of seeking to accentuate and define. What was apparently being brought about by discursive efforts, and in a mighty controversy and confusion, is coming about now as a matter of course.

Before the war, in the British community as in most civilized communities, profound changes were already in progress, changes in the conditions of women's employment, in the legal relations of husband and wife, in the political status of women, in the status of illegitimate children, in manners and customs affecting the sexes. Every civilized community was exhibiting a falling birth-rate and a falling death-rate, was changing the quality of its housing, and diminishing domestic labour by organising supplies and developing, appliances. That is to say, that primary human unit, the home, was altering in shape and size and frequency and colour and effect. A steadily increasing proportion of people were living outside the old family home, the home based on maternity and offspring, altogether. A number of us were doing our best to apprehend the summation of all this flood of change. We had a vague idea that women were somehow being "emancipated," but just what this word meant and what it implied were matters still under exploration. Then came the war. For a time it seemed as if all this discussion was at an end, as if the problem itself had vanished.

But that was only a temporary distraction of attention. The process of change swirled into new forms that did not fit very easily into the accepted formulae, swirled into new forms and continued on its way. If the discussion ceased for a time, the process of change ceased not at all. Matters have travelled all the farther in the last two years for travelling mutely. The questions between men and women are far more important and far more incessant than the questions between Germans and the rest of mankind. They are coming back now into the foreground of human thought, but amended and altered. Our object is to state the general nature of that alteration. It has still been "emancipation," but very different in quality from the "emancipation" that was demanded so loudly and incoherently in that ancient world—of 1913!

Never had the relations of men and women been so uneasy as they were in the opening days of 1914. The woman's movement battered and banged through all our minds. It broke out into that tumult in Great Britain perhaps ten years ago. When Queen Victoria died it was inaudible; search *Punch*, search the newspapers of that tranquil age. In 1914 it kicked up so great a dust that the Germans counted on the Suffragettes as one of the great forces that were to paralyse England in the war.

The extraordinary thing was that the feminist movement was never clearly defined during all the time of its maximum violence. We begin to perceive in the retrospect that the movement was multiple, made up of a number of very different movements interwoven. It seemed to concentrate upon the Vote; but it was never possible to find even why women wanted the vote. Some, for example, alleged that it was because they were like men, and some because they were entirely different. The broad facts that one could not mistake were a vast feminine discontent and a vast display of feminine energy. What had brought that about?

Two statistical factors are to be considered here. One of these was the steady decline in the marriage rate, and the increasing proportion of unmarried women of all classes, but particularly of the more educated classes, requiring employment. The second was the fall in the birth-rate, the diminution in size of the average family, the increase of sterile unions, and the consequent release of a considerable proportion of the energy of married women. Co-operating with these factors of release were the economic elaborations that were improving the appliances of domestic life, replacing the needle by the sewing machine, the coal fire and lamp by gas and electricity, the dustpan and brush by the pneumatic carpet cleaner, and taking out of the house into the shop and factory the baking, much of the cooking, the making of clothes, the laundry work, and so forth, that had hitherto kept so many women at home and too busy to think. The care of even such children as there were was

H. G. Wells

also less arduous; creche and school held out hands for them, ready to do even that duty better.

Side by side with these releases from duty was a rise in the standard of education that was stimulating the minds and imaginations of woman beyond a point where the needle—even if there had been any use for the needle—can be an opiate. Moreover, the world was growing richer, and growing richer in such a way that not only were leisure and desire increasing, but, because of increasingly scientific methods of production, the need in many branches of employment for any but very keen and able workers was diminishing. So that simultaneously the world, that vanished world before 1914, was releasing and disengaging enormous volumes of untrained and unassigned feminine energy and also diminishing the usefulness of unskilful effort in every department of life. There was no demand to meet the supply. These were the underlying processes that produced the feminist outbreak of the decade before the war.

Now the debate between the sexes is a perennial. It began while we were still in the trees. It has its stereotyped accusations; its stereotyped repartees. The Canterbury Pilgrims had little to learn from Christabel Pankhurst. Man and woman in that duet struggle perpetually for the upper hand, and the man restrains the woman and the woman resents the man. In every age some voice has been heard asserting, like Plato, that the woman is a human being; and the prompt answer has been, "but such a different human being." Wherever there is a human difference fair play is difficult, the universal clash of races witnesses to that, and sex is the greatest of human differences.

But the general trend of mankind towards intelligence and reason has been also a trend away from a superstitious treatment of sexual questions and a recognition, so to speak, that a woman's "a man for a' that," that she is indeed as entitled to an independent soul and a separate voice in collective affairs. As brain has counted for more and more in the human effort and brute strength and the advantage of not bearing children for less and less, as man has felt a greater need for a companion and a lesser need for a slave, and as the increase of food and the protection of the girl from premature child-bearing has approximated the stature and strength and enterprise of the woman more and more to that of the man, this secular emancipation of the human female from the old herd subordination and servitude to the patriarchal male has gone on. Essentially the secular process has been an equalising process. It was merely the exaggeration of its sustaining causes during the plenty and social and intellectual expansion of the last half-century that had stimulated this secular process to the pitch of crisis.

There have always been two extreme aspects of the sexual debate. There have always been the oversexed women who wanted to be treated primarily as women, and the women who were irritated and bored by being treated primarily as women. There have always been those women who wanted to get, like Joan of Arc, into masculine attire, and the school of the "mystical darlings." There have always been the women who wanted to share men's work and the women who wanted to "inspire" it—the mates and the mistresses. Of course, the mass of women lies between these extremes. But it is possible, nevertheless, to discuss this question as though it were a conflict of two sharply opposed ideals. It is convenient to write as if there were just these two sorts of women because so one can get a sharp definition in the picture. The ordinary woman fluctuates between the two, turns now to the Western ideal of citizenship and now to the Eastern of submission. These ideals fight not only in human society, but in every woman's career.

Chitra in Rabindranath Tagore's play, for example, tried both aspects of the woman's life, and Tagore is at one with Plato in preferring the Rosalind type to the houri. And with him I venture to think is the clear reason of mankind. The real "emancipation" to which reason and the trend of things makes is from the yielding to the energetic side of a woman's disposition, from beauty enthroned for love towards the tall, weather-hardened woman with a spear, loving her mate as her mate loves her, and as sexless as a man in all her busy hours.

But it was not simply the energies that tended towards this particular type that were set free during the latter half of the nineteenth century. Every sort of feminine energy was set free. And it was not merely the self-reliant, independence-seeking women who were discontented. The ladies who specialised in feminine arts and graces and mysteries were also dissatisfied. They found they were not important enough. The former type found itself insufficiently respected, and the latter type found itself insufficiently adored. The two mingled their voices in the most confusing way in the literature of the suffrage movement before the war. The two tendencies mingle confusingly in the minds of the women that this movement was stirring up to think. The Vote became the symbol for absolutely contradictory things; there is scarcely a single argument for it in suffragist literature that cannot be completely negatived out of suffragist literature.

For example, compare the writings of Miss Cicely Hamilton, the distinguished actress, with the publications of the Pankhurst family. The former expresses a claim that, except for prejudice, a woman is as capable a citizen as a man and differing only in her sex; the latter consist of a long rhapsody upon the mystical superiorities of women and the marvellous benefits mankind will derive from handing things over to these sacred powers. The former would get rid of sex from most human affairs; the latter would make what our Georgian grandfathers called "The Sex" rule the world.

Or compare, say, the dark coquettings of Miss Elizabeth Robins' "Woman's Secret" with the virile common sense of that most brilliant young writer, Miss Rebecca West, in her bitter onslaught on feminine limitations in the opening chapters of "The World's Worst Failure." The former is an extravagance of sexual mysticism. Man can never understand women. Women always hide deep and wonderful things away beyond masculine discovery. Men do not even suspect. Some day, perhaps—It is someone peeping from behind a curtain, and inviting men in provocative tones to come and play catch in a darkened harem. The latter is like some gallant soldier cursing his silly accoutrements. It is a hearty outbreak against that apparent necessity for elegance and sexual specialisation that undercuts so much feminine achievement, that reduces so much feminine art and writing to vapidity, and holds back women from the face of danger and brave and horrible deaths. It is West to Miss Robins' East. And yet I believe I am right in saying that all these four women writers have jostled one another upon suffrage platforms, and that they all suffered blows and injuries in the same cause, during the various riots and conflicts that occurred in London in the course of the great agitation. It was only when the agitation of the Pankhurst family, aided by Miss Robins' remarkable book "Where are you going to ...?" took a form that threatened to impose the most extraordinary restrictions on the free movements of women, and to establish a sort of universal purdah of hostility and suspicion against those degraded creatures, those stealers and destroyers of women, "the men," that the British feminist movement displayed any tendency to dissociate into its opposed and divergent strands.

It is a little detail, but a very significant one in this connection, that the committee that organised the various great suffrage processions in London were torn by dispute about the dresses of the processionists. It was urged that a "masculine style of costume" discredited the movement, and women were urged to dress with a maximum of feminine charm. Many women obtained finery they could ill afford, to take part in these demonstrations, and minced their steps as womanly as possible to freedom....

It would be easy to overstate the efflorescence of distinctively feminine emotion, dressiness, mysticism, and vanity upon the suffrage movement. Those things showed for anyone to see. This was the froth of the whirlpool. What did not show was the tremendous development of the sense of solidarity among women. Everybody knew that women had been hitting policemen at Westminster; it was not nearly so showy a fact that women of title, working women, domestic servants, tradesmen's wives, professional workers, had all been meeting together and working together in a common cause, working with an unprecedented capacity and an unprecedented disregard of social barriers. One noted the nonsensical by-play of the movement; the way in which women were accustoming themselves to higher standards of achievement was not so immediately noticeable. That a small number of women were apparently bent on rendering the Vote impossible by a campaign of violence and malicious mischief very completely masked the fact that a very great number of girls and young women no longer considered it seemly to hang about at home trying by a few crude inducements to tempt men to marry them, but were setting out very seriously and capably to master the young man's way of finding a place for oneself in the world. Beneath the dust and noise realities were coming about that the dust and noise entirely failed to represent. We know that some women were shrieking for the Vote; we did not realise that a generation of women was qualifying for it.

The war came, the jolt of an earthquake, to throw things into their proper relationships.

The immediate result was the disappearance of the militant suffragists from public view for a time, into which the noisier section hastened to emerge in full scream upon the congenial topic of War Babies. "Men," those dreadful creatures, were being camped and quartered all over the country. It followed, from all the social principles known to Mrs. And Miss Pankhurst, that it was necessary to provide for an enormous number of War Babies. Subscriptions were invited. Statisticians are still looking rather perplexedly for those War Babies; the illegitimate birth-rate has fallen, and what has become of the subscriptions I do not know. *The Suffragette* rechristened itself *Britannia*, dropped the War Baby agitation, and, after an interlude of self-control, broke out into denunciations, first of this public servant and then of that, as traitors and German spies. Finally, it discovered a mare's nest in the case of Sir Edward Grey that led to its suppression, and the last I have from this misleading and unrepresentative feminist faction is the periodic appearance of a little ill-printed sheet of abuse about the chief Foreign Office people, resembling in manner and appearance the sort of denunciatory letter, at once suggestive and evasive, that might be written by the curate's discharged cook. And with that the aggressive section of the suffragist movement seems to have petered out, leaving the broad reality of feminine emancipation to go on in a beneficent silence.

There can be no question that the behaviour of the great mass of women in Great Britain has not simply exceeded expectation but hope. And there can be as little doubt that the suffrage question, in spite of the self-advertising violence of its extravagant section, did contribute very materially to build up the confidence, the willingness to undertake responsibility and face hardship, that has been so abundantly displayed by every class of woman. It is not simply that there has been enough women and to spare for hospital work and every sort of relief and charitable service; that sort of thing has been done before, that was in the tradition of womanhood. It is that at every sort of occupation, clerking, shop-keeping, railway work, automobile driving, agricultural work, police work, they have been found efficient beyond precedent and intelligent beyond precedent. And in the munition factories, in the handling of heavy and often difficult machinery, and in adaptability and inventiveness and enthusiasm and steadfastness their achievement has been astonishing. More particularly in relation to intricate mechanical work is their record remarkable and unexpected.

There is scarcely a point where women, having been given a chance, have not more than made good. They have revolutionised the estimate of their economic importance, and it is scarcely too much to say that when, in the long run, the military strength of the Allies bears down the strength of Germany, it will be this superiority of our women which enables us to pit a woman at—the censorship will object to exact geography upon this point—against a man at Essen which has tipped the balance of this war.

Those women have won the vote. Not the most frantic outbursts of militancy after this war can prevent them getting it. The girls who have faced death and wounds so gallantly in our cordite factories—there is a not inconsiderable list of dead and wounded from those places—have killed for ever the poor argument that women should not vote because they had no military value. Indeed, they have killed every argument against their subjection. And while they do these things, that paragon of the virtues of the old type, that miracle of domestic obedience, the German *haus-frau*, the faithful Gretchen, riots for butter.

And as I have before remarked, the Germans counted on the suffragettes as one of the great forces that were to paralyse England in this war.

It is not simply that the British women have so bountifully produced intelligence and industry; that does not begin their record. They have been willing to go dowdy. The mass of women in Great Britain are wearing the clothes of 1914. In 1913 every girl and woman one saw in the streets of London had an air of doing her best to keep in the fashion. Now they are for the most part as carelessly dressed as a busy business man or a clever young student might have been. They are none the less pretty for that, and far more beautiful. But the fashions have floated away to absurdity. Every now and then through the austere bustle of London in war time drifts a last practitioner of the "eternal feminine"—with the air of a foreign visitor, with the air of devotion to some peculiar cult. She has very high-heeled boots; she shows a leg, she has a short skirt with a peculiar hang, due no doubt to mysteries about the waist; she wears a comic little hat over one brow; there is something of Columbine about her, something of the Watteau shepherdess, something of a vivandiere, something of every age but the present age. Her face, subject to the strange dictates of the mode, is smooth like the back of a spoon, with small features and little whisker-like curls before the ears such as butcher-boys used to wear half a century ago. Even so, she dare not do this thing alone. Something in khaki is with her, to justify her. You are to understand that this strange rig is for seeing him off or giving him a good time during his leave. Sometimes she is quite elderly, sometimes nothing khaki is to be got, and the pretence that this is desired of her wears thin. Still, the type will out.

She does not pass with impunity, the last exponent of true feminine charm. The vulgar, the street boy, have evolved one of those strange sayings that have the air of being fragments from some lost and forgotten chant:

"She's the Army Contractor's Only Daughter, Spending it now."

Or simply, "Spending it now."

She does not pass with impunity, but she passes. She makes her stilted passage across the arena upon which the new womanhood of Western Europe shows its worth. It is an exit. There is likely to be something like a truce in the fashions throughout Europe for some years. It is in America if anywhere that the holy fires of smartness and the fashion will be kept alive....

And so we come to prophecy.

I do not believe that this invasion by women of a hundred employments hitherto closed to them is a temporary arrangement that will be reversed after the war. It is a thing that was going on, very slowly, it is true, and against much prejudice and opposition, before the war, but it was going on; it is in the nature of things. These women no doubt enter these employments as substitutes, but not usually as inferior substitutes; in quite a number of cases they are as good as men, and in many they are not underselling, they are drawing men's pay. What reason is there to suppose that they will relapse into a state of superfluous energy after the war? The war has merely brought about, with the rapidity of a landslide, a state of affairs for which the world was ripe. The world after the war will have to adjust itself to this extension of women's employment, and to this increase in the proportion of self-respecting, self-supporting women.

Contributing very largely to the establishment of this greatly enlarged class of independent women will be the great shortage for the next decade of marriageable men, due to the killing and disablement of the war. The women of the next decades will not only be able to get along economically without marriage, but they will find it much more difficult to marry. It will also probably be a period in which a rise in prices may, as it usually does, precede the compensating rise in wages. It may be that for some years it will be more difficult to maintain a family. This will be a third factor in the fixation of this class of bachelor women.

Various writers, brooding over the coming shortage of men, have jumped to the conclusion that polygamy is among the probabilities of the near future. They write in terms of real or affected alarm for which there is no justification; they wallow in visions of Germany "legalising" polygamy, and see Berlin seeking recuperation, in man power by converting herself into another Salt Lake City. But I do not think that Germany, in the face of the economic ring that the Allies will certainly draw about her, is likely to desire a very great increase in population for the next few years; I do not see any great possibility of a specially rich class capable of maintaining numerous wives being sustained by the impoverished and indebted world of Europe, nor the sources from which a supply of women preferring to become constituents in a polygamous constellation rather than self-supporting freewomen is to be derived.

The temperamental dislike of intelligent women to polygamy is at least as strong as a man's objection to polyandry. Polygamy, open or hidden, flourishes widely only where there are women to be bought. Moreover, there are considerable obstacles in religion and custom to be overcome by the innovating polygamist—even in Germany. It might mean a breach of the present good relations between Germany and the Vatican. The relative inferiority of the tradition of the German to that of most other European women, its relative disposition towards feminine servitude, is no doubt a consideration on the other scale of this discussion, but I do not think it is one heavy enough to tilt back the beam.

So far from a great number of men becoming polygamists, I think it would be possible to show cause for supposing that an increasing proportion will cease even to be monogamists. The romantic excitements of the war have produced a temporary rise in the British marriage rate; but before the war it had been falling slowly and the average age at marriage had been rising, and it is quite possible that this process will be presently resumed and, as a new generation grows up to restore the balance of the sexes, accelerated.

We conclude, therefore, that this increase in the class of economically independent bachelor women that is now taking place is a permanent increase. It is probably being reinforced by a considerable number of war widows who will not remarry. We have to consider in what directions this mass of capable, intelligent, energetic, undomesticated freewomen is likely to develop, what its effect will be on social usage, and particularly how it will react upon the lives of the married women about them. Because, as we have already pointed out in this chapter, the release of feminine energy upon which the feminist problem depends is twofold, being due not only to the increased unmarriedness of women through the disproportion of the sexes and the rise in the age of marriage, but also to the decreased absorption of married women in domestic duties. A woman, from the point of view of this discussion, is not "married and done for," as she used to be. She is not so extensively and completely married. Her large and increasing leisure remains in the problem.

The influence of this coming body of freewomen upon the

general social atmosphere will be, I venture to think, liberalising and relaxing in certain directions and very bracing in others. This new type of women will want to go about freely without an escort, to be free to travel alone, take rooms in hotels, sit in restaurants, and so forth. Now, as the women of the past decade showed, there are for a woman two quite antagonistic ways of going about alone. Nothing showed the duplicate nature of the suffragist movement more than the great variety of deportment of women in the London streets during that time. There were types that dressed neatly and quietly and went upon their business with intent and preoccupied faces. Their intention was to mingle as unobtrusively as possible into the stream of business, to be as far as possible for the ordinary purposes of traffic "men in a world of men." A man could speak to such women as he spoke to another man, without suspicion, could, for example, ask his way and be directed without being charged with annoying or accosting a delicate female.

At the other extreme there was a type of young woman who came into the streets like something precious that has got loose. It dressed itself as feminine loveliness; it carried sex like a banner and like a challenge. Its mind was fully prepared by the Pankhurst literature for insult. It swept past distressed manhood imputing motives. It was pure hareem, and the perplexed masculine intelligence could never determine whether it was out for a demonstration or whether it was out for a spree. Its motives in thus marching across the path of feminine emancipation were probably more complicated and confused than that alternative suggests, and sheer vanity abounded in the mixture. But undoubtedly that extremity is the vanishing extremity of these things. The new freewoman is going to be a grave and capable being, soberly dressed, and imposing her own decency and neutrality of behaviour upon the men she meets. And along the line of sober costume and simple and restrained behaviour that the freewoman is marking out, the married woman will also escape to new measures of freedom.

I do not believe that among women of the same social origins and the same educational quality there can exist side by side entirely distinct schools of costume, deportment, and behaviour based on entirely divergent views of life. I do not think that men can be trained to differentiate between different sorts of women, sorts of women they will often be meeting simultaneously, and to treat this one with frankness and fellowship and that one with awe passion and romantic old-world gallantry. All sorts of intermediate types—the majority of women will be intermediate types—will complicate the problem. This conflict of the citizen-woman ideal with the loveliness-woman ideal, which was breaking out very plainly in the British suffrage movement before the war, will certainly return after the war, and I have little doubt which way the issue will fall. The human being is going to carry it against the sexual being. The struggle is going to be extensive and various and prolonged, but in the serious years ahead the serious type must, I feel, win. The plain, well-made dress will oust the ribbon and the decolletage.

In every way the war is accelerating the emancipation of women from sexual specialisation. It is facilitating their economic emancipation. It is liberating types that will inevitably destroy both the "atmosphere of gallantry" which is such a bar to friendliness between people of opposite sexes and that atmosphere of hostile distrust which is its counterpart in the minds of the over-sexual suffragettes. It is arresting the change of fashions and simplifying manners.

In another way also it is working to the same end. That fall in the birth-rate which has been so marked a feature in the social development of all modern states has become much more perceptible since the war began to tell upon domestic comfort. There is a full-cradle agitation going on in Germany to check this decline; German mothers are being urged not to leave the Crown Prince of 1930 or 1940 without the necessary material for glory at some fresh Battle of Verdun. I doubt the zeal of their response. But everywhere the war signifies economic stress which must necessarily continue long after the war is over, and in the present state of knowledge that stress means fewer children. The family, already light, will grow lighter. This means that marriage, although it may be by no means less emotionally sacred, will become a lighter thing.

Once, to be married was a woman's whole career. Household cares, a dozen children, and she was consumed. All her romances ended in marriage. All a decent man's romance ended there, too. She proliferated and he toiled, and when the married couple had brought up some of their children and buried the others, and blessed their first grandchildren, life was over.

Now, to be married is an incident in a woman's career, as in a man's. There is not the same necessity of that household, not the same close tie; the married woman remains partially a freewoman and assimilates herself to the freewoman. There is an increasing disposition to group solitary children and to delegate their care to specially qualified people, and this is likely to increase, because the high earning power of young women will incline them to entrust their children to others, and because a shortage of men and an excess of widows will supply other women willing to undertake that care. The more foolish women will take these releases as a release into levity, but the common sense of the newer types of women will come to the help of men in recognising the intolerable nuisance of this prolongation of flirting and charming on the part of people who have had what should be a satisfying love.

Nor will there be much wealth or superfluity to make levity possible and desirable. Winsome and weak womanhood will be told bluntly by men and women alike that it is a bore. The frou-frou of skirts, the delicate mysteries of the toilette, will cease to thrill any but the very young men. Marriage, deprived of its bonds of material necessity, will demand a closer and closer companionship as its justification and excuse. A marriage that does not ripen into a close personal friendship between two equals will be regarded with increasing definiteness as an unsatisfactory marriage.

These things are not stated here as being desirable or undesirable. This is merely an attempt to estimate the drift and tendency of the time as it has been accentuated by the war. It works out to the realisation that marriage is likely to count for less and less as a state and for more and more as a personal relationship. It is likely to be an affair of diminishing public and increasing private importance. People who marry are likely to remain, so far as practical ends go, more detached and separable. The essential link will be the love and affection and not the home.

With that go certain logical consequences. The first is that the circumstances of the unmarried mother will resemble more than they have hitherto done those of many married mothers; the harsh lines once drawn between them will dissolve. This will fall in with the long manifest tendency in modern society to lighten the disadvantages (in the case of legacy duties, for example) and stigma laid upon illegitimate children. And a type of marriage where personal compatibility has come to be esteemed the fundamental thing will be altogether more amenable to divorce than the old union which was based upon the kitchen and the nursery, and the absence of any care, education, or security for children beyond the range of the parental household. Marriage will not only be lighter, but more dissoluble.

To summarise all that has gone before, this war is accelerating rather than deflecting the stream of tendency, and is bringing us rapidly to a state of affairs in which women will be much more definitely independent of their sexual status, much less hampered in their self-development, and much more nearly equal to men than has ever been known before in the whole history of mankind....

H. G. Wells

IX

THE NEW MAP OF EUROPE

Section 1

In this chapter it is proposed to embark upon what may seem now, with the Great War still in progress and still undecided, the most hopeless of all prophetic adventures. This is to speculate upon the redrawing of the map of Europe after the war. But because the detailed happenings and exact circumstances of the ending of the war are uncertain, they need not alter the inevitable broad conclusion. I have already discussed that conclusion, and pointed out that the war has become essentially a war of mutual exhaustion. This does not mean, as some hasty readers may assume, that I foretell a "draw." We may be all white and staggering, but Germany is, I believe, fated to go down first. She will make the first advances towards peace; she will ultimately admit defeat.

But I do want to insist that by that time every belligerent, and not simply Germany, will be exhausted to a pitch of extreme reasonableness. There will be no power left as Germany was left in 1871, in a state of "freshness' and a dictatorial attitude. That is to say they will all be gravitating, rot to triumphs, but to such a settlement as seems to promise the maximum of equilibrium in the future.

If towards the end of the war the United States should decide, after all, to abandon their present attitude of superior comment and throw their weight in favour of such a settlement as would make the recrudescence of militarism impossible, the general exhaustion may give America a relative importance far beyond any influence she could exert at the present time. In the end, America may have the power to insist upon almost vital conditions in the settlement; though whether she will have the imaginative force and will is, of course, quite another question.

And before I go on to speculate about the actual settlement, there are one or two generalisations that it may be interesting to try over. Law is a thin wash that we paint over the firm outlines of reality, and the treaties and agreements of emperors and kings and statesmen have little of the permanence of certain more fundamental human realities. I was looking the other day at Sir Mark Sykes' "The Caliph's Inheritance," which contains a series of coloured maps of the political boundaries of south-western Asia for the last three thousand years. The shapes and colours come and go—now it is Persia, now it is Macedonia, now the Eastern Empire, now the Arab, now the Turk who is ascendant. The colours change as if they were in a kaleidoscope; they advance, recede, split, vanish. But through all that time there exists obstinately an Armenia, an essential Persia, an Arabia; they, too, advance or recede a little. I do not claim that they are eternal things, but they are far more permanent things than any rulers or empires; they are rooted to the ground by a peasantry, by a physical and temperamental attitude. Apart from political maps of mankind, there are natural maps of mankind. I find it, too, in Europe; the monarchs splash the water and break up the mirror in endless strange shapes; nevertheless, always it is tending back to its enduring forms; always it is gravitating back to a Spain, to a Gaul, to an Italy, to a Serbo-Croatia, to a Bulgaria, to a Germany, to a Poland. Poland and Armenia and Egypt destroyed, subjugated, invincible, I would take as typical of what I mean by the natural map of mankind.

Let me repeat again that I do not assert there is an eternal map.

It does change; there have been times—the European settlement of America and Siberia, for example, the Arabic sweep across North Africa, the invasion of Britain by the Low German peoples—when it has changed very considerably in a century or so; but at its swiftest it still takes generations to change. The gentlemen who used to sit in conferences and diets, and divide up the world ever and again before the nineteenth century, never realised this. It is only within the last hundred years that mankind has begun to grasp the fact that one of the first laws of political stability is to draw your political boundaries along the lines of the natural map of mankind.

Now the nineteenth century phrased this conception by talking about the "principle of nationality." Such interesting survivals of the nineteenth century as Mr. C.R. Buxton still talk of settling human affairs by that "principle." But unhappily for him the world is not so simply divided. There are tribal regions with no national sense. There are extensive regions of the earth's surface where the population is not homogeneous, where people of different languages or different incompatible creeds live village against village, a kind of human emulsion, incapable of any true mixture or unity. Consider, for example, Central Africa, Tyrone, Albania, Bombay, Constantinople or Transylvania. Here are regions and cities with either no nationality or with as much nationality as a patchwork quilt has colour....

Now so far as the homogeneous regions of the world go, I am quite prepared to sustain the thesis that they can only be tranquil, they can only develop their possibilities freely and be harmless to their neighbours, when they are governed by local men, by men of the local race, religion and tradition, and with a form of government that, unlike a monarchy or a plutocracy, does not crystallise commercial or national ambition. So far I go with those who would appeal to the "principle of nationality."

But I would stipulate, further, that it would enormously

increase the stability of the arrangement if such "nations" could be grouped together into "United States" wherever there were possibilities of inter-state rivalries and commercial friction. Where, however, one deals with a region of mixed nationality, there is need of a subtler system of adjustments. Such a system has already been worked out in the case of Switzerland, where we have the community not in countries but cantons, each with its own religion, its culture and self-government, and all at peace under a polyglot and impartial common government. It is as plain as daylight to anyone who is not blinded by patriotic or private interests that such a country as Albania, which is mono-lingual indeed, but hopelessly divided religiously, will never be tranquil, never contented, unless it is under a cantonal system, and that the only solution of the Irish difficulty along the belt between Ulster and Catholic Ireland lies in the same arrangement.

Then; thirdly, there are the regions and cities possessing no nationality, such as Constantinople or Bombay, which manifestly appertain not to one nation but many; the former to all the Black Sea nations, the latter to all India. Disregarding ambitions and traditions, it is fairly obvious that such international places would be best under the joint control of, and form a basis of union between, all the peoples affected.

Now it is suggested here that upon these threefold lines it is possible to work out a map of the world of maximum contentment and stability, and that there will be a gravitation of all other arrangements, all empires and leagues and what not, towards this rational and natural map of mankind. This does not imply that that map will ultimately assert itself, but that it will always be tending to assert itself. It will obsess ostensible politics.

I do not pretend to know with any degree of certainty what peculiar forms of muddle and aggression may not record themselves upon the maps of 2200; I do not certainly know whether mankind will be better off or worse off then, more or less civilised; but I do know, with a very considerable degree of

H. G. Wells

certainty, that in A.D. 2200 there will still be a France, an Ireland, a Germany, a Jugo-Slav region, a Constantinople, a Rajputana, and a Bengal. I do not mean that these are absolutely fixed things; they may have receded or expanded. But these are the more permanent things; these are the field, the groundwork, the basic reality; these are fundamental forces over which play the ambitions, treacheries, delusions, traditions, tyrannies of international politics. All boundaries will tend to reveal these fundamental forms as all clothing tends to reveal the body. You may hide the waist; you will only reveal the shoulders the more. You may mask, you may muffle the body; it is still alive inside, and the ultimate determining thing.

And, having premised this much, it is possible to take up the problem of the peace of 1917 or 1918, or whenever it is to be, with some sense of its limitations and superficiality.

We have already hazarded the prophecy that after a long war of general exhaustion Germany will be the first to realise defeat. This does not mean that she will surrender unconditionally, but that she will be reduced to bargaining to see how much she must surrender, and what she may hold. It is my impression that she will be deserted by Bulgaria, and that Turkey will be out of the fighting before the end. But these are chancy matters. Against Germany there will certainly be the three great allies, France, Russia and Britain, and almost certainly Japan will be with them. The four will probably have got to a very complete and detailed understanding among themselves. Italy—in, I fear, a slightly detached spirit—will sit at the board. Hungary will be present, sitting, so to speak, amidst the decayed remains of Austria. Roumania, a little out of breath through hurrying at the last, may be present as the latest ally of Italy. The European neutrals will be at least present in spirit; their desires will be acutely felt; but it is doubtful if the United States will count for all that they might in the decision. Such weight as America chooses to exercise—would that she would choose to exercise more!—will probably be on the side of the rational and natural settlement of the world.

Now the most important thing of all at this settlement will be the temper and nature of the Germany with which the Allies will be dealing. Let us not be blinded by the passions of war into confusing a people with its government and the artificial Kultur of a brief century. There is a Germany, great and civilised, a decent and admirable people, masked by Imperialism, blinded by the vanity of the easy victories of half a century ago, wrapped in illusion. How far will she be chastened and disillusioned by the end of this war?

The terms of peace depend enormously upon the answer to that question. If we take the extremest possibility, and suppose a revolution in Germany or in South Germany, and the replacement of the Hohenzollerns in all or part of Germany by

H. G. Wells

a Republic, then I am convinced that for republican Germany there would be not simply forgiveness, but a warm welcome back to the comity of nations. The French, British, Belgians and Italians, and every civilised force in Russia would tumble over one another in their eager greeting of this return to sanity.

If we suppose a less extreme but more possible revolution, taking the form of an inquiry into the sanity of the Kaiser and his eldest son, and the establishment of constitutional safeguards for the future, that also would bring about an extraordinary modification of the resolution of the Pledged Allies. But no ending to this war, no sort of settlement, will destroy the antipathy of the civilised peoples for the violent, pretentious, sentimental and cowardly imperialism that has so far dominated Germany. All Europe outside Germany now hates and dreads the Hohenzollerns. No treaty of peace can end that hate, and so long as Germany sees fit to identify herself with Hohenzollern dreams of empire and a warfare of massacre and assassination, there must be war henceforth, open, or but thinly masked, against Germany. It will be but the elementary common sense of the situation for all the Allies to plan tariffs, exclusions, special laws against German shipping and shareholders and immigrants for so long a period as every German remains a potential servant of that system.

Whatever Germany may think of the Hohenzollerns, the world outside Germany regards them as the embodiment of homicidal nationalism. And the settlement of Europe after the war, if it is to be a settlement with the Hohenzollerns and not with the German people, must include the virtual disarming of those robber murderers against any renewal of their attack. It would be the most obvious folly to stop anywhere short of that. With Germany we would welcome peace to-morrow; we would welcome her shipping on the seas and her flag about the world; against the Hohenzollerns it must obviously be war to the bitter end.

But the ultimate of all sane European policy, as distinguished from oligarchic and dynastic foolery, is the establishment of the natural map of Europe. There exists no school of thought that can claim a moment's consideration among the Allies which aims at the disintegration of the essential Germany or the subjugation of any Germans to an alien rule. Nor does anyone grudge Germany wealth, trade, shipping, or anything else that goes with the politician's phrase of "legitimate expansion" for its own sake. If we do now set our minds to deprive Germany of these things in their fullness, it is in exactly the same spirit as that in which one might remove that legitimate and peaceful implement, a bread knife, from the hand of a homicidal maniac. Let but Germany cure herself of her Hohenzollern taint, and the world will grudge her wealth and economic pre-eminence as little as it grudges wealth and economic pre-eminence to the United States.

Now the probabilities of a German revolution open questions too complex and subtle for our present speculation. I would merely remark in passing that in Great Britain at least those possibilities seem to me to be enormously underrated. For our present purpose it will be most convenient to indicate a sort of maximum and minimum, depending upon the decision of Germany to be entirely Hohenzollern or wholly or in part European. But in either case we are going to assume that it is Germany which has been most exhausted by the war, and which is seeking peace from the Allies, who have also, we will assume, excellent internal reasons for desiring it.

With the Hohenzollerns it is mere nonsense to dream of any enduring peace, but whether we are making a lasting and friendly peace with Germany or merely a sort of truce of military operations that will be no truce in the economic war against Hohenzollern resources, the same essential idea will, I think, guide all the peace-desiring Powers. They will try to draw the boundaries as near as they can to those of the natural map of mankind.

Then, writing as an Englishman, my first thought of the European map is naturally of Belgium. Only absolute smashing defeat could force either Britain or France to consent to anything short of the complete restoration of Belgium. Rather than give that consent they will both carry the war to at present undreamt-of extremities. Belgium must be restored; her neutrality must be replaced by a defensive alliance with her two Western Allies; and if the world has still to reckon with Hohenzollerns, then her frontier must be thrust forward into the adjacent French-speaking country so as to minimise the chances of any second surprise.

It is manifest that every frontier that gives upon the Hohenzollerns must henceforth be entrenched line behind line, and held permanently by a garrison ready for any treachery, and it becomes of primary importance that the Franco-Belgian line should be as short and strong as possible. Aix, which Germany has made a mere jumping-off place for aggressions, should clearly be held by Belgium against a Hohenzollern Empire, and the fortified and fiscal frontier would run from it southward to include the Grand Duchy of Luxembourg, with its French sympathies and traditions, in the permanent alliance. It is quite impossible to leave this ambiguous territory as it was before the war, with its railway in German hands and its postal and telegraphic service (since 1913) under Hohenzollern control. It is quite impossible to hand over this strongly anti-Prussian population to Hohenzollern masters.

But an Englishman must needs write with diffidence upon this question of the Western boundary. It is clear that all the boundaries of 1914 from Aix to Bale are a part of ancient history. No "as you were" is possible there. And it is not the business of anyone in Great Britain to redraw them. That task on our side lies between France and Belgium. The business of Great Britain in the matter is as plain as daylight. It is to support to her last man and her last ounce of gold those new boundaries her allies consider essential to their comfort and security.

But I do not see how France, unless she is really convinced she is beaten, can content herself with anything less than a strong

Franco-Belgian frontier from Aix, that will take in at least Metz and Saarburg. She knows best the psychology of the lost provinces, and what amount of annexation will spell weakness or strength. If she demands all Alsace-Lorraine back from the Hohenzollerns, British opinion is resolved to support her, and to go through with this struggle until she gets it. To guess at the direction of the new line is not to express a British opinion, but to speculate upon the opinion of France. After the experience of Luxembourg and Belgium no one now dreams of a neutralized buffer State. What does not become French or Belgian of the Rhineland will remain German—for ever. That is perhaps conceivable, for example, of Strassburg and the low-lying parts of Alsace. I do not know enough to do more than guess.

It is conceivable, but I do not think that it is probable. I think the probability lies in the other direction. This war of exhaustion may be going on for a year or so more, but the end will be the thrusting in of the too extended German lines. The longer and bloodier the job is, the grimmer will be the determination of the Pledged Allies to exact a recompense. If the Germans offer peace while they still hold some part of Belgium, there will be dealings. If they wait until the French are in the Palatinate, then I doubt if the French will consent to go again. There will be no possible advantage to Germany in a war of resistance once the scale of her fortunes begins to sink....

It is when we turn to the east of Germany that the map-drawing becomes really animated. Here is the region of great decisions. The natural map shows a line of obstinately non-German communities, stretching nearly from the Baltic to the Adriatic. There are Poland, Bohemia (with her kindred Slovaks), the Magyars, and the Jugo-Serbs. In a second line come the Great and Little Russians, the Roumanians, and the Bulgarians. And here both Great Britain and France must defer to the wishes of their two allies, Russia and Italy. Neither of these countries has expressed inflexible intentions, and the situation has none of the inevitable quality of the Western line. Except for the Tsar's promise of autonomy to Poland, nothing

H. G. Wells

has been promised. On the Western line there are only two possibilities that I can see: the Aix-Bale boundary, or the sickness and death of France. On the Eastern line nothing is fated. There seems to be enormous scope for bargaining over all this field, and here it is that the chances of compensations and consolations for Germany are to be found.

Let us first consider the case for Poland. The way to a reunited Poland seems to me a particularly difficult one. The perplexity arises out of the crime of the original partition; whichever side emerges with an effect of victory must needs give up territory if an autonomous Poland is to reappear. A victorious Germany would probably reconstitute the Duchy of Warsaw under a German prince; an entirely victorious Russia would probably rejoin Posen to Russian Poland and the Polish fragment of Galicia, and create a dependent Polish kingdom under the Tsar. Neither project would be received with unstinted delight by the Poles, but either would probably be acceptable to a certain section of them. Disregarding the dim feelings of the peasantry, Austrian Poland would probably be the most willing to retain a connection with its old rulers. The Habsburgs have least estranged the Poles. The Cracow district is the only section of Poland which has been at all reconciled to foreign control; it is the most autonomous and contented of the fragments.

It is doubtful how far national unanimity is any longer possible between the three Polish fragments. Like most English writers, I receive a considerable amount of printed matter from various schools of Polish patriotism, and wide divergences of spirit and intention appear. A weak, divided and politically isolated Poland of twelve or fifteen million people, under some puppet adventurer king set up between the Hohenzollerns and the Tsardom, does not promise much happiness for the Poles or much security for the peace of the world. An entirely independent Poland will be a feverish field of international intrigue—intrigue to which the fatal Polish temperament lends itself all too readily; it may be a battlefield again within five-and-twenty years. I think, if I were a patriotic Pole, I should determine to be a Slav at any cost, and make the best of Russia; ally myself with all her liberal tendencies, and rise or fall with her. And I should do my utmost in a field where at present too little has been done to establish understandings and lay the foundations of a future alliance with the Czech-Slovak community to the south. But, then, I am not a Pole, but a Western European with a strong liking for the Russians. I am democratic and scientific, and the Poles I have met are Catholic and aristocratic and romantic, and all sorts of difficult things that must make co-operation with them on the part of Russians, Ruthenian peasants, Czechs, and, indeed, other Poles, slow and insecure. I doubt if either Germany or Russia wants to incorporate more Poles—Russia more particularly, which has all Siberia over which to breed Russians—and I am inclined to think that there is a probability that the end of this war may find Poland still divided, and with boundary lines running across her not materially different from those of 1914. That is, I think, an undesirable probability, but until the Polish mind qualifies its desire for absolute independence with a determination to orient itself definitely to some larger political mass, it remains one that has to be considered.

But the future of Poland is not really separate from that of the Austro-Hungarian monarchy, nor is that again to be dealt with apart from that of the Balkans. From Danzig to the Morea there runs across Europe a series of distinctive peoples, each too intensely different and national to be absorbed and assimilated by either of their greater neighbours, Germany or Russia, and each relatively too small to stand securely alone. None have shaken themselves free from monarchical traditions; each may become an easy prey to dynastic follies and the aggressive obsessions of diplomacy. Centuries of bloody rearrangement may lie before this East Central belt of Europe.

To the liberal idealist the thought of a possible Swiss system or group of Swiss systems comes readily to mind. One thinks of a grouping of groups of Republics, building up a United States of Eastern Europe. But neither Hohenzollerns nor Tsar would

H. G. Wells

welcome that. The arm of democratic France is not long enough to reach to help forward such a development, and Great Britain is never sure whether she is a "Crowned Republic" or a Germanic monarchy. Hitherto in the Balkans she has lent her influence chiefly to setting up those treacherous little German kings who have rewarded her so ill. The national monarchs of Serbia and Montenegro have alone kept faith with civilisation. I doubt, however, if Great Britain will go on with that dynastic policy. She herself is upon the eve of profound changes of spirit and internal organisation. But whenever one thinks of the possibilities of Republican development in Europe as an outcome of this war, it is to realise the disastrous indifference of America to the essentials of the European situation. The United States of America could exert an enormous influence at the close of the war in the direction of a liberal settlement and of liberal institutions.... They will, I fear, do nothing of the sort.

It is here that the possibility of some internal change in Germany becomes of such supreme importance. The Hohenzollern Imperialism towers like the black threat of a new Caesarism over all the world. It may tower for some centuries; it may vanish to-morrow. A German revolution may destroy it; a small group of lunacy commissioners may fold it up and put it away. But should it go, it would at least take with it nearly every crown between Hamburg and Constantinople. The German kings would vanish like a wisp of smoke. Suppose a German revolution and a correlated step forward towards liberal institutions on the part of Russia, then the whole stage of Eastern Europe would clear as fever goes out of a man. This age of international elbowing and jostling, of intrigue and diplomacy, of wars, massacres, deportations *en masse*, and the continual fluctuation of irrational boundaries would come to an end forthwith.

So sweeping a change is the extreme possibility. The probability is of something less lucid and more prosaic; of a discussion of diplomatists; of patched arrangements. But even under these circumstances the whole Eastern European situation is so fluid and little controlled by any plain necessity, that there will be enormous scope for any individual statesman of imagination and force of will.

There have recently been revelations, more or less trustworthy, of German schemes for a rearrangement of Eastern Europe. They implied a German victory. Bohemia, Poland, Galicia and Ruthenia were to make a Habsburg-ruled State from the Baltic to the Black Sea. The Jugo-Slav and the Magyar were to be linked (uneasy bedfellows) into a second kingdom, also Habsburg ruled; Austria was to come into the German Empire as a third Habsburg dukedom or kingdom; Roumania, Bulgaria and Greece were to continue as independent Powers, German ruled. Recently German proposals published in America have shown a disposition to admit the claims of Roumania to the Wallachian districts of Transylvania.

Evidently the urgent need to create kingdoms or confederations larger than any such single States as the natural map supplies, is manifest to both sides. If Germany, Italy and Russia can come to any sort of general agreement in these matters, their arrangements will be a matter of secondary importance to the Western Allies—saving our duty to Serbia and Montenegro and their rulers. Russia may not find the German idea of a Polish *plus* Bohemian border State so very distasteful, provided that the ruler is not a German; Germany may find the idea still tolerable if the ruler is not the Tsar.

The destiny of the Serbo-Croatian future lies largely in the hands of Italy and Bulgaria. Bulgaria was not in this war at the beginning, and she may not be in it at the end. Her King is neither immortal nor irreplaceable. Her desire now must be largely to retain her winnings in Macedonia, and keep the frontier posts of a too embracing Germany as far off as possible. She has nothing to gain and much to fear from Roumania and Greece. Her present relations with Turkey are unnatural. She has everything to gain from a prompt recovery of the friendship of Italy and the sea Powers. A friendly Serbo-Croatian buffer State against Germany will probably be of

H. G. Wells

equal comfort in the future to Italy and Bulgaria; more especially if Italy has pushed down the Adriatic coast along the line of the former Venetian possessions. Serbia has been overrun, but never were the convergent forces of adjacent interests so clearly in favour of her recuperation. The possibility of Italy and that strange Latin outlier, Roumania, joining hands through an allied and friendly Serbia must be very present in Italian thought. The allied conception of the land route from the West and America to Bagdad and India is by Mont Cenis, Trieste, Serbia and Constantinople, as their North European line to India is through Russia by Baku.

And that brings us to Constantinople.

Constantinople is not a national city; it is now, and it has always been, an artificial cosmopolis, and Constantinople and the Dardanelles are essentially the gate of the Black Sea. It is to Russia that the waterway is of supreme importance. Any other Power upon it can strangle Russia; Russia, possessing it, is capable of very little harm to any other country.

Roumania is the next most interested country. But Roumania can reach up the Danube and through Bulgaria, Serbia or Hungary to the outer world. Her greatest trade will always be with Central Europe. For generations the Turks held Thrace and Anatolia before they secured Constantinople. The Turk can exist without Constantinople; he is at his best outside Constantinople; the fall of Constantinople was the beginning of his decay. He sat down there and corrupted. His career was at an end. I confess that I find a bias in my mind for a Russian ownership of Constantinople. I think that if she does not get it now her gravitation towards it in the future will be so great as to cause fresh wars. Somewhere she must get to open sea, and if it is not through Constantinople then her line must lie either through a dependent Armenia thrust down to the coast of the Levant or, least probable and least desirable of all, through the Persian Gulf. The Constantinople route is the most natural and least controversial of these. With the dwindling of the Turkish power, the Turks at Constantinople become more and more like robber knights levying toll at the pass. I can imagine Russia making enormous concessions in Poland, for example, accepting retrocessions, and conceding autonomy, rather than foregoing her ancient destiny upon the Bosphorus. I believe she will fight on along the Black Sea coast until she gets there.

This, I think, is Russia's fundamental end, without which no peace is worth having, as the liberation of Belgium and the satisfaction of France is the fundamental end of Great Britain, and Trieste-Fiume is the fundamental end of Italy.

But for all the lands that lie between Constantinople and West Prussia there are no absolutely fundamental ends; that is the land of *quid pro quo*; that is where the dealing will be done. Serbia must be restored and the Croats liberated; sooner or later the south Slav state will insist upon itself; but, except for that, I see no impossibility in the German dream of three kingdoms to take the place of Austro-Hungary, nor even in a southward extension of the Hohenzollern Empire to embrace the German one of the three. If the Austrians have a passion for Prussian "kultur," it is not for us to restrain it. Austrian, Saxon, Bavarian, Hanoverian and Prussian must adjust their own differences. Hungary would be naturally Habsburg; is, in fact, now essentially Habsburg, more Habsburg than Austria, and essentially anti-Slav. Her gravitation to the Central Powers seems inevitable.

Whether the Polish-Czech combination would be a Habsburg kingdom at all is another matter. Only if, after all, the Allies are far less successful than they have now every reason to hope would that become possible.

The gravitation of that west Slav state to the Central European system or to Russia will, I think, be the only real measure of ultimate success or failure in this war. I think it narrows down to that so far as Europe is concerned. Most of the other things are inevitable. Such, it seems to me, is the most open possibility in the European map in the years immediately before us.

H. G. Wells

If by dying I could assure the end of the Hohenzollern Empire to-morrow I would gladly do it. But I have, as a balancing prophet, to face the high probability of its outliving me for some generations. It is to me a deplorable probability. Far rather would I anticipate Germany quit of her eagles and Hohenzollerns, and ready to take her place as the leading Power of the United States of Europe.

X

THE UNITED STATES, FRANCE, BRITAIN, AND RUSSIA

Section 1

In this chapter I propose to speculate a little about the future development of these four great States, whose destinies are likely to be much more closely interwoven than their past histories have been. I believe that the stars in their courses tend to draw these States together into a dominant peace alliance, maintaining the peace of the world. There may be other stars in that constellation, Italy, Japan, a confederated Latin America, for example; I do not propose to deal with that possibility now, but only to dwell upon the development of understandings and common aims between France, Russia, and the English-speaking States.

They have all shared one common experience during the last two years; they have had an enormous loss of self-sufficiency. This has been particularly the case with the United States of America. At the beginning of this war, the United States were still possessed by the glorious illusion that they were aloof from general international politics, that they needed no allies and need fear no enemies, that they constituted a sort of asylum from war and all the bitter stresses and hostilities of the old world. Themselves secure, they could intervene with grim resolution to protect their citizens all over the world. Had they

H. G. Wells

not bombarded Algiers?...

I remember that soon after the outbreak of the war I lunched at the Savoy Hotel in London when it was crammed with Americans suddenly swept out of Europe by the storm. My host happened to be a man of some diplomatic standing, and several of them came and talked to him. They were full of these old-world ideas of American immunity. Their indignation was comical even at the time. Some of them had been hustled; some had lost their luggage in Germany. When, they asked, was it to be returned to them? Some seemed to be under the impression that, war or no war, an American tourist had a perfect right to travel about in the Vosges or up and down the Rhine just as he thought fit. They thought he had just to wave a little American flag, and the referee would blow a whistle and hold up the battle until he had got by safely. One family had actually been careering about in a cart—their automobile seized—between the closing lines of French and Germans, brightly unaware of the disrespect of bursting shells for American nationality.... Since those days the American nation has lived politically a hundred years.

The people of the United States have shed their delusion that there is an Eastern and a Western hemisphere, and that nothing can ever pass between them but immigrants and tourists and trade, and realised that this world is one round globe that gets smaller and smaller every decade if you measure it by day's journeys. They are only going over the lesson the British have learnt in the last score or so of years. This is one world and bayonets are a crop that spreads. Let them gather and seed, it matters not how far from you, and a time will come when they will be sticking up under your nose. There is no real peace but the peace of the whole world, and that is only to be kept by the whole world resisting and suppressing aggression wherever it arises. To anyone who watches the American Press, this realisation has been more and more manifest. From dreams of aloofness and ineffable superiority, America comes round very rapidly to a conception of an active participation in the difficult business of statecraft. She is thinking of alliances, of throwing her weight and influence upon the side of law and security. No longer a political Thoreau in the woods, a sort of vegetarian recluse among nations, a being of negative virtues and unpremeditated superiorities, she girds herself for a manly part in the toilsome world of men.

So far as I can judge, the American mind is eminently free from any sentimental leaning towards the British. Americans have a traditional hatred of the Hanoverian monarchy, and a democratic disbelief in autocracy. They are far more acutely aware of differences than resemblances. They suspect every Englishman of being a bit of a gentleman and a bit of a flunkey. I have never found in America anything like that feeling common in the mass of English people that prevents the use of the word "foreigner" for an American; there is nothing to reciprocate the sympathy and pride that English and Irish republicans and radicals feel for the States. Few Americans realise that there are such beings as English republicans.

What has linked Americans with the British hitherto has been very largely the common language and literature; it is only since the war began that there seems to have been any appreciable development of fraternal feeling. And that has been not so much discovery of a mutual affection as the realisation of a far closer community of essential thought and purpose than has hitherto been suspected. The Americans, after thinking the matter out with great frankness and vigour, do believe that Britain is on the whole fighting against aggression and not for profit, that she is honestly backing France and Belgium against an intolerable attack, and that the Hohenzollern Empire is a thing that needs discrediting and, if possible, destroying in the interests of all humanity, Germany included.

America has made the surprising discovery that, allowing for their greater nearness, the British are thinking about these things almost exactly as Americans think about them. They

H. G. Wells

follow the phases of the war in Great Britain, the strain, the blunderings, the tenacity, the onset of conscription in an essentially non-military community, with the complete understanding of a people similarly circumstanced, differing only by scale and distance. They have been through something of the sort already; they may have something of the sort happen again. It had not occurred to them hitherto how parallel we were. They begin to have inklings of how much more parallel we may presently become.

There is evidence of a real search for American affinities among the other peoples of the world; it is a new war-made feature of the thoughtful literature and journalists of America. And it is interesting to note how partial and divided these affinities must necessarily be. Historically and politically, the citizen of the United States must be drawn most closely to France. France is the one other successful modern republic; she was the instigator and friend of American liberation. With Great Britain the tie of language, the tradition of personal freedom, and the strain in the blood are powerful links. But both France and Britain are old countries, thickly populated, with a great and ancient finish and completeness, full of implicit relationships; America is by comparison crude, uninformed, explicit, a new country, still turning fresh soil, still turning over but half-explored natural resources.

The United States constitute a modern country, a country on an unprecedented scale, being organised from the very beginning on modern lines. There is only one other such country upon the planet, and that curiously enough is parallel in climate, size, and position—Russia in Asia. Even Russia in Europe belongs rather to the newness that is American than to the tradition that is European; Harvard was founded more than half a century before Petrograd. And when I looked out of the train window on my way to Petrograd from Germany, the little towns I saw were like no European towns I had ever seen. The wooden houses, the broad unmade roads, the traffic, the winter-bitten scenery, a sort of untidy spaciousness, took my mind instantly to the country one sees in the back part of

New York State as one goes from Boston to Niagara. And the reality follows the appearance.

The United States and Russia are the west and the east of the same thing; they are great modern States, developing from the beginning upon a scale that only railways make possible. France and Britain may perish in the next two centuries or they may persist, but there can be no doubt that two centuries ahead Russia and the United States will be two of the greatest masses of fairly homogeneous population on the globe.

There are no countries with whom the people of the United States are so likely to develop sympathy and a sense of common values and common interests as with these three, unless it be with the Scandinavian peoples. The Scandinavian peoples have developed a tendency to an extra-European outlook, to look west and east rather than southwardly, to be pacifist and progressive in a manner essentially American. From any close sympathy with Germany the Americans are cut off at present by the Hohenzollerns and the system of ideas that the Hohenzollerns have imposed upon German thought. So long as the Germans cling to the tawdry tradition of the Empire, so long as they profess militarism, so long as they keep up their ridiculous belief in some strange racial superiority to the rest of mankind, it is absurd to expect any co-operative feeling between them and any other great people.

The American tradition is based upon the casting off of a Germanic monarchy; it is its cardinal idea. These sturdy Republicans did not fling out the Hanoverians and their Hessian troops to prepare the path of glory for Potsdam. But except for the gash caused by the Teutonic monarchy, there runs round the whole world a north temperate and sub-arctic zone of peoples, generally similar in complexion, physical circumstances, and intellectual and moral quality, having enormous undeveloped natural resources, and a common interest in keeping the peace while these natural resources are developed, having also a common interest in maintaining the integrity of China and preventing her development into a military power; it is a zone with the clearest prospect of a vast increase in its already enormous population, and it speaks in the main one or other of three languages, either French, Russian, or English. I believe that natural sympathy will march with the obvious possibilities of the situation in bringing the American mind to the realisation of this band of common interests and of its compatibility with the older idea of an American continent protected by a Monroe doctrine from any possibility of aggression from the monarchies of the old world.

As the old conception of isolation fades and the American mind accustoms itself to the new conception of a need of alliances and understandings to save mankind from the megalomania of races and dynasties, I believe it will turn first to the idea of keeping the seas with Britain and France, and then to this still wider idea of an understanding with the Pledged Allies that will keep the peace of the world.

Now Germany has taught the world several things, and one of the most important of these lessons is the fact that the destinies of states and peoples is no longer to be determined by the secret arrangements of diplomatists and the agreements or jealousies of kings. For fifty years Germany has been unifying the mind of her people against the world. She has obsessed them with an evil ideal, but the point we have to note is that she has succeeded in obsessing them with that ideal. No other modern country has even attempted such a moral and mental solidarity as Germany has achieved. And good ideals need, just as much as bad ones, systematic inculcation, continual open expression and restatement. Mute, mindless, or demented nations are dangerous and doomed nations. The great political conceptions that are needed to establish the peace of the world must become the common property of the mass of intelligent adults if they are to hold against the political scoundrel, the royal adventurer, the forensic exploiter, the enemies and scatterers of mankind. The French, Americans, and English have to realise this necessity; they have to state a common will and they have to make their possession by that will understood by the Russian people, and they have to share that will with the Russian people. Beyond that there lies the still greater task or making some common system of understandings with the intellectual masses of China and India. At present, with three of these four great powers enormously preoccupied with actual warfare, there is an opportunity for guiding expression on the part of America, for a real world leadership, such as may never occur again....

So far I have been stating a situation and reviewing certain possibilities. In the past half-century the United States has been developing a great system of universities and a continental production of literature and discussion to supplement the limited Press and the New England literature of the earlier phase of the American process. It is one of the most interesting speculations in the world to everyone how far this new organisation of the American mind is capable of grasping the stupendous opportunities and appeals of the present time. The war and the great occasions that must follow the war will tax the mind and the intellectual and moral forces of the Pledged Allies enormously. How far is this new but very great and growing system of thought and learning in the United States capable of that propaganda of ideas and language, that progressive expression of a developing ideal of community, that in countries so spontaneous, so chaotic or democratic as the United States and the Pledged Allies must necessarily take the place of the organised authoritative *Kultur* of the Teutonic type of state?

As an undisguisedly patriotic Englishman, I would like to see the lead in this intellectual synthesis of the nations, that *must* be achieved if wars are to cease, undertaken by Great Britain. But I am bound to confess that in Great Britain I see neither the imaginative courage of France nor the brisk enterprise of the Americans. I see this matter as a question of peace and civilisation, but there are other baser but quite as effective reasons why America, France, and Great Britain should exert themselves to create confidences and understandings between their populations and the Russian population. There is the immediate business opportunity in Russia. There is the secondary business opportunity in China that can best be developed as the partners rather than as the rivals of the Russians. Since the Americans are nearest, by way of the Pacific, since they are likely to have more capital and more free energy to play with than the Pledged Allies, I do on the whole incline to the belief that it is they who will yet do the pioneer work and the leading work that this opportunity demands.

If beneath the alliances of the present war there is to grow up a system of enduring understandings that will lead to the peace of the world, there is needed as a basis for such understandings much greater facility of intellectual intercourse than exists at present. Firstly, the world needs a *lingua franca*; next, the Western peoples need to know more of the Russian language and life than they do, and thirdly, the English language needs to be made more easily accessible than it is at present. The chief obstacle to a Frenchman or Englishman learning Russian is the difficult and confusing alphabet; the chief obstacle to anyone learning English is the irrational spelling. Are people likely to overcome these very serious difficulties in the future, and, if so, how will they do it? And what prospects are there of a *lingua franca*?

Wherever one looks closely into the causes and determining influences of the great convulsions of this time, one is more and more impressed by the apparent smallness of the ultimate directing influence. It seems to me at least that it is a practically proven thing that this vast aggression of Germany is to be traced back to a general tone of court thinking and discussion in the Prussia of the eighteenth century, to the theories of a few professors and the gathering trend of German education in a certain direction. It seems to me that similarly the language teachers of to-day and to-morrow may hold in their hands the seeds of gigantic international developments in the future.

It is not a question of the skill or devotion of individual teachers so much as of the possibility of organising them upon a grand scale. An individual teacher must necessarily use the ordinary books and ordinary spelling and type of the language in which he is giving instruction; he may get a few elementary instruction books from a private publisher, specially printed for teaching purposes, but very speedily he finds himself obliged to go to the current printed matter. This, as I will

H. G. Wells

immediately show, bars the most rapid and fruitful method of teaching. And in this as in most affairs, private enterprise, the individualistic system, shows itself a failure. In England, for example, the choice of Russian lesson books is poor and unsatisfactory, and there is either no serviceable Russian-English, English-Russian school dictionary in existence, or it is published so badly as to be beyond the range of my inquiries. But a state, or a group of universities, or even a rich private association such as far-seeing American, French and British business men might be reasonably expected to form, could attack the problem of teaching a language in an altogether different fashion.

The difficulty in teaching English lies in the inconsistency of the spelling, and the consequent difficulties of pronunciation. If there were available an ample series of text-books, reading books, and books of general interest, done in a consistent phonetic type and spelling—in which the value of the letters of the phonetic system followed as far as possible the prevalent usage in Europe—the difficulty in teaching English not merely to foreigners but, as the experiments in teaching reading of the Simplified Spelling Society have proved up to the hilt, to English children can be very greatly reduced. At first the difficulty of the irrational spelling can be set on one side. The learner attacks and masters the essential language. Then afterwards he can, if he likes, go on to the orthodox spelling, which is then no harder for him to read and master than it is for an Englishman of ordinary education to read the facetious orthography of Artemus Ward or of the *Westminster Gazette* "orfis boy." The learner does one thing at a time instead of attempting, as he would otherwise have to do, two things—and they are both difficult and different and conflicting things—simultaneously.

Learning a language is one thing and memorising an illogical system of visual images—for that is what reading ordinary English spelling comes to—is quite another. A man can learn to play first chess and then bridge in half the time that these two games would require if he began by attempting simultaneous play, and exactly the same principle applies to the language problem.

These considerations lead on to the idea of a special development or sub-species of the English language for elementary teaching and foreign consumption. It would be English, very slightly simplified and regularised, and phonetically spelt. Let us call it Anglo-American. In it the propagandist power, whatever that power might be, state, university or association, would print not simply, instruction books but a literature of cheap editions. Such a specialised simplified Anglo-American variety of English would enormously stimulate the already wide diffusion of the language, and go far to establish it as that *lingua franca* of which the world has need.

And in the same way, the phonetic alphabet adopted as the English medium could be used as the medium for instruction in French, where, as in the British Isles, Canada, North and Central Africa, and large regions of the East, it is desirable to make an English-speaking community bi-lingual. At present a book in French means nothing to an uninstructed Englishman, an English book conveys no accurate sound images to an uninstructed Frenchman. On the other hand, a French book printed on a proper phonetic system could be immediately read aloud—though of course it could not be understood—by an uninstructed Englishman. From the first he would have no difficulties with the sounds. And vice versa. Such a system of books would mean the destruction of what are, for great masses of French and English people, insurmountable difficulties on the way to bi-lingualism. Its production is a task all too colossal for any private publishers or teachers, but it is a task altogether trivial in comparison with the national value of its consequences. But whether it will ever be carried out is just one of those riddles of the jumping cat in the human brain that are most perplexing to the prophet.

The problem becomes at once graver, less hopeful, and more urgent when we take up the case of Russian. I have looked closely into this business of Russian teaching, and I am convinced that only a very, very small number of French-and English-speaking people are going to master Russian under the existing conditions of instruction. If we Westerns want to get at Russia in good earnest we must take up this Russian language problem with an imaginative courage and upon a scale of which at present I see no signs. If we do not, then the Belgians, French, Americans and English will be doing business in Russia after the war in the German language—or through a friendly German interpreter. That, I am afraid, is the probability of the case. But it need not be the case. Will and intelligence could alter all that.

What has to be done is to have Russian taught at first in a Western phonetic type. Then it becomes a language not very much more difficult to acquire than, say, German by a Frenchman. When the learner can talk with some freedom, has a fairly full vocabulary, a phraseology, knows his verb and so on, then and then only should he take up the unfamiliar and confusing set of visual images of Russian lettering—I speak from the point of view of those who read the Latin alphabet. How confusing it may be only those who have tried it can tell. Its familiarity to the eye increases the difficulty; totally unfamiliar forms would be easier to learn. The Frenchman or Englishman is confronted with

COP;

the sound of that is

SAR!

For those who learn languages, as so many people do nowadays, by visual images, there will always be an undercurrent toward saying "COP." The mind plunges hopelessly through that tangle to the elements of a speech which is as yet unknown.

Nevertheless almost all the instruction in Russian of which I can get an account begins with the alphabet, and must, I suppose, begin with the alphabet until teachers have a suitably printed set of instruction books to enable them to take the better line. One school teacher I know, in a public school, devoted the entire first term, the third of a year, to the alphabet. At the end he was still dissatisfied with the progress of his pupils. He gave them Russian words, of course, words of which they knew nothing—in Russian characters. It was too much for them to take hold of at one and the same time. He did not even think of teaching them to write French and English words in the strange lettering. He did not attempt to write his Russian in Latin letters. He was apparently ignorant of any system of transliteration, and he did nothing to mitigate the impossible task before him. At the end of the term most of his pupils gave up the hopeless effort. It is not too much to say that for a great number of "visualising" people, the double effort at the outset of Russian is entirely too much. It stops them altogether. But to almost anyone it is possible to learn Russian if at first it is presented in a lettering that gives no trouble.

If I found myself obliged to learn Russian urgently, I would get some accepted system of transliteration, carefully transcribe every word of Russian in my text-book into the Latin characters, and learn the elements of the language from my manuscript. A year or so ago I made a brief visit to Russia with a "Russian Self-Taught" in my pocket. Nothing sticks, nothing ever did stick of that self-taught Russian except the words that I learnt in Latin type. Those I remember as I remember all words, as groups of Latin letters. I learnt to count, for example, up to a hundred. The other day I failed to recognise the Russian word for eleven in Russian characters until I had spelt it out. Then I said, "Oh, of course!" But I knew it when I heard it.

I write of these things from the point of view of the keen learner. Some Russian teachers will be found to agree with me; others will not. It is a paradox in the psychology of the teacher that few teachers are willing to adopt "slick" methods of teaching; they hate cutting corners far more than they hate obstacles, because their interest is in the teaching and not in the "getting there." But what we learners want is not an exquisite, rare knowledge of particulars, we do not want to spend an hour upon Russian needlessly; we want to get there as quickly and effectively as possible. And for that, transliterated books are essential.

Now these may seem small details in the learning of languages, mere schoolmasters' gossip, but the consequences are on the continental scale. The want of these national text-books and readers is a great gulf between Russia and her Allies; *it is a greater gulf than the profoundest political misunderstanding could be*. We cannot get at them to talk plainly to them, and they cannot get at us to talk plainly to us. A narrow bridge of interpreters is our only link with the Russian mind. And many of those interpreters are of a race which is for very good reasons hostile to Russia. An abundant cheap supply, firstly, of English and French books, *in* English and French, but in the Russian character, by means of which Russians may rapidly learn French and English—for it is quite a fable that these languages are known and used in Russia below the level of the court and aristocracy—and, secondly, of Russian books in the Latin (or some easy phonetic development of the Latin) type, will do more to facilitate interchange and intercourse between Russia and France, America and Britain, and so consolidate the present alliance than almost any other single thing. But that supply will not be a paying thing to provide; if it is left to publishers or private language teachers or any form of private enterprise it will never be provided. It is a necessary public undertaking.

But because a thing is necessary it does not follow that it will be achieved. Bread may be necessary to a starving man, but there is always the alternative that he will starve. France, which is most accessible to creative ideas, is least interested in this particular matter. Great Britain is still heavily conservative. It is idle to ignore the forces still entrenched in the established church, in the universities and the great schools, that stand for an irrational resistance to all new things. American universities are comparatively youthful and sometimes quite surprisingly innovating, and America is the country of the adventurous millionaire. There has been evidence in several American papers that have reached me recently of a disposition to get ahead with Russia and cut out the Germans (and incidentally the British). Amidst the cross-currents and overlappings of this extraordinary time, it seems to me highly probable that America may lead in this vitally important effort to promote international understanding.

H. G. Wells

XI

"THE WHITE MAN'S BURTHEN"

One of the most curious aspects of the British "Pacifist" is his willingness to give over great blocks of the black and coloured races to the Hohenzollerns to exploit and experiment upon. I myself being something of a pacifist, and doing what I can, in my corner, to bring about the Peace of the World, the Peace of the World triumphant and armed against every disturber, could the more readily sympathise with the passive school of Pacifists if its proposals involved the idea that England should keep to England and Germany to Germany. My political ideal is the United States of the World, a union of states whose state boundaries are determined by what I have defined as the natural map of mankind. I cannot understand those pacifists who talk about the German right to "expansion," and babble about a return of her justly lost colonies. That seems to me not pacificism but patriotic inversion. This large disposition to hand over our fellow-creatures to a Teutonic educational system, with "frightfulness" in reserve, to "efficiency" on Wittenberg lines, leaves me—hot. The ghosts of the thirst-tormented Hereros rise up in their thousands from the African dust, protesting.

This talk of "legitimate expansion" is indeed now only an exploiter's cant. The age of "expansion," the age of European "empires" is near its end. No one who can read the signs of the times in Japan, in India, in China, can doubt it. It ended in America a hundred years ago; it is ending now in Asia; it will end last in Africa, and even in Africa the end draws near. Spain has but led the way which other "empires" must follow. Look at her empire in the atlases of 1800. She fell down the steps violently and painfully, it is true—but they are difficult to descend. No sane man, German or anti-German, who has weighed the prospects of the new age, will be desirous of a restoration of the now vanished German colonial empire, vindictive, intriguing, and unscrupulous, a mere series of centres of attack upon adjacent territory, to complicate the immense disentanglements and readjustments that lie already before the French and British and Italians.

Directly we discuss the problem of the absolutely necessary permanent alliance that this war has forced upon at least France, Belgium, Britain and Russia, this problem of the "empires" faces us. What are these Allies going to do about their "subject races"? What is the world going to do about the "subject races"? It is a matter in which the "subject races" are likely to have an increasingly important voice of their own. We Europeans may discuss their fate to-day among ourselves; we shall be discussing it with them to-morrow. If we do not agree with them then, they will take their fates in their own hands in spite of us. Long before A.D. 2100 there will be no such thing as a "subject race" in all the world.

Here again we find ourselves asking just that same difficult question of more or less, that arises at every cardinal point of our review of the probable future. How far is this thing going to be done finely; how far is it going to be done cunningly and basely? How far will greatness of mind, how far will imaginative generosity, prevail over the jealous and pettifogging spirit that lurks in every human being? Are French and British and Belgians and Italians, for example, going to help each other in Africa, or are they going to work against and cheat each other? Is the Russian seeking only a necessary outlet to the seas of the world, or has he dreams of Delhi? Here again, as in all these questions, personal idiosyncrasy comes in; I am strongly disposed to trust the good in the Russian.

H. G. Wells

But apart from this uncertain question of generosity, there are in this case two powerful forces that make against disputes, secret disloyalties, and meanness. One is that Germany will certainly be still dangerous at the end of the war, and the second is that the gap in education, in efficiency, in national feeling and courage of outlook, between the European and the great Asiatic and African communities, is rapidly diminishing. If the Europeans squabble much more for world ascendancy, there will be no world ascendancy for them to squabble for. We have still no means of measuring the relative enfeeblement of Europe in comparison with Asia already produced by this war. As it is, certain things are so inevitable—the integration of a modernised Bengal, of China, and of Egypt, for example— that the question before us is practically reduced to whether this restoration of the subject peoples will be done with the European's aid and goodwill, or whether it will be done against him. That it will be done in some manner or other is certain.

The days of suppression are over. They know it in every country where white and brown and yellow mingle. If the Pledged Allies are not disposed to let in light to their subject peoples and prepare for the days of world equality that are coming, the Germans will. If the Germans fail to be the most enslaving of people, they may become the most liberating. They will set themselves, with their characteristic thoroughness, to destroy that magic "prestige" which in Asia particularly is the clue to the miracle of European ascendancy. In the long run that may prove no ill service to mankind. The European must prepare to make himself acceptable in Asia, to state his case to Asia and be understood by Asia, or to leave Asia. That is the blunt reality of the Asiatic situation.

It has already been pointed out in these chapters that if the alliance of the Pledged Allies is indeed to be permanent, it implies something in the nature of a Zollverein, a common policy towards the rest of the world and an arrangement involving a common control over the dependencies of all the Allies. It will be interesting, now that we have sketched a possible map of Europe after the war, to look a little more closely into the nature of the "empires" concerned, and to attempt a few broad details of the probable map of the Eastern hemisphere outside Europe in the years immediately to come.

Now there are, roughly speaking, three types of overseas "possessions." They may be either (1) territory that was originally practically unoccupied and that was settled by the imperial people, or (2) territory with a barbaric population having no national idea, or (3) conquered states. In the case of the British Empire all three are present; in the case of the French only the second and third; in the case of the Russian only the first and third. Each of these types must necessarily follow its own system of developments. Take first those territories originally but thinly occupied, or not occupied at all, of which all or at least the dominant element of the population is akin to that of the "home country." These used to be called by the British "colonies"—though the "colonies" of Greece and Rome were really only garrison cities settled in foreign lands—and they are now being rechristened "Dominions." Australia, for instance, is a British Dominion, and Siberia and most of Russia in Asia, a Russian Dominion. Their manifest destiny is for their children to become equal citizens with the cousins and brothers they have left at home.

There has been much discussion in England during the last decade upon some modification of the British legislature that would admit representatives from the Dominions to a proportional share in the government of the Empire. The problem has been complicated by the unsettled status of Ireland and the mischief-making Tories there, and by the perplexities arising out of those British dependencies of non-British race—the Indian states, for example, whose interests are sometimes in conflict with those of the Dominions.

The attractiveness of the idea of an Imperial legislature is chiefly on the surface, and I have very strong doubts of its realisability. These Dominions seem rather to tend to become independent and distinct sovereign states in close and affectionate alliance with Great Britain, and having a common interest in the British Navy. In many ways the interests of the Dominions are more divergent from those of Great Britain than are Great Britain and Russia, or Great Britain and France. Many of the interests of Canada are more closely bound to those of the United States than they are to those of Australasia, in such a matter as the maintenance of the Monroe Principle, for example. South Africa again takes a line with regard to British Indian subjects which is highly embarrassing to Great Britain. There is a tendency in all the British colonies to read American books and periodicals rather than British, if for no other reason than because their common life, life in a newish and very democratic land, is much more American than British in character.

On the other hand, one must remember that Great Britain has European interests—the integrity of Holland and Belgium is a case in point—which are much closer to the interests of France than they are to those of the younger Britains beyond the seas. A voice in an Alliance that included France and the United States, and had its chief common interest in the control of the seas, may in the future seem far more desirable to these great and growing English-speaking Dominions than the sending of representatives to an Imperial House of Lords at Westminster, and the adornment of elderly colonial politicians with titles and decorations at Buckingham Palace.

I think Great Britain and her Allies have all of them to prepare their minds for a certain release of their grip upon their "possessions," if they wish to build up a larger unity; I do not see that any secure unanimity of purpose is possible without such releases and readjustments.

Now the next class of foreign "possession" is that in which the French and Belgians and Italians are most interested. Britain also has possessions of this type in Central Africa and the less civilized districts of India, but Russia has scarcely anything of the sort. In this second class of possession the population is numerous, barbaric, and incapable of any large or enduring political structure, and over its destinies rule a small minority of European administrators.

The greatest of this series of possessions are those in black Africa. The French imagination has taken a very strong hold of the idea of a great French-speaking West and Central Africa, with which the ordinary British citizen will only too gladly see the conquered German colonies incorporated. The Italians have a parallel field of development in the hinterland of Tripoli. Side by side, France, Belgium and Italy, no longer troubled by hostile intrigues, may very well set themselves in the future to the task of building up a congenial Latin civilisation out of the tribal confusions of these vast regions. They will, I am convinced, do far better than the English in this domain. The English-speaking peoples have been perhaps the most successful *settlers* in the world; the United States and the Dominions are there to prove it; only the Russians in Siberia can compare with them; but as administrators the British are a race coldly aloof. They have nothing to give a black people, and no disposition to give.

The Latin-speaking peoples, the Mediterranean nations, on the other hand, have proved to be the most successful *assimilators* of other races that mankind has ever known. Alexandre Dumas is not the least of the glories of France. In a hundred years' time black Africa, west of Tripoli, from Oran to Rhodesia, will, I believe, talk French. And what does not speak French will speak the closely related Italian. I do not see why this Latin black culture should not extend across equatorial Africa to meet the Indian influence at the coast, and reach out to join hands with Madagascar. I do not see why the British flag should be any impediment to the Latinisation of tropical Africa or to the natural extension of the French and Italian languages through Egypt. I guess, however, that it will be an Islamic and not a Christian cult that will be talking Italian and French. For the French-speaking civilisation will make roads not only for French, Belgians, and Italians, but for the Arabs whose religion and culture already lie like a net over black Africa. No other peoples and no other religion can so conveniently give the negro what is needed to bring him into

H. G. Wells

the comity of civilized peoples....

A few words of digression upon the future of Islam may not be out of place here. The idea of a militant Christendom has vanished from the world. The last pretensions of Christian propaganda have been buried in the Balkan trenches. A unification of Africa under Latin auspices carries with it now no threat of missionary invasion. Africa will be a fair field for all religions, and the religion to which the negro will take will be the religion that best suits his needs. That religion, we are told by nearly everyone who has a right to speak upon such questions, is Islam, and its natural propagandist is the Arab. There is no reason why he should not be a Frenchified Arab.

Both the French and the British have the strongest interest in the revival of Arabic culture. Let the German learn Turkish if it pleases him. Through all Africa and Western Asia there is a great to-morrow for a renascent Islam under Arab auspices. Constantinople, that venal city of the waterways, sitting like Asenath at the ford, has corrupted all who came to her; she has been the paralysis of Islam. But the Islam of the Turk is a different thing from the Islam of the Arab. That was one of the great progressive impulses in the world of men. It is our custom to underrate the Arab's contribution to civilisation quite absurdly in comparison with our debt to the Hebrew and Greek. It is to the initiatives of Islamic culture, for example, that we owe our numerals, the bulk of modern mathematics, and the science of chemistry. The British have already set themselves to the establishment of Islamic university teaching in Egypt, but that is the mere first stroke of the pick at the opening of the mine. English, French, Russian, Arabic, Hindustani, Spanish, Italian; these are the great world languages that most concern the future of civilisation from the point of view of the Peace Alliance that impends. No country can afford to neglect any of those languages, but as a matter of primary importance I would say, for the British, Hindustani, for the Americans, Russian or Spanish, for the French and Belgians and Italians, Arabic. These are the directions in which the duty of understanding is most urgent for each of these peoples, and the path of opportunity plainest.

The disposition to underrate temporarily depressed nations, races, and cultures is a most irrational, prevalent, and mischievous form of stupidity. It distorts our entire outlook towards the future. The British reader can see its absurdity most easily when he reads the ravings of some patriotic German upon the superiority of the "Teuton" over the Italians and Greeks—to whom we owe most things of importance in European civilisation. Equally silly stuff is still to be read in British and American books about "Asiatics." And was there not some fearful rubbish, not only in German but in English and French, about the "decadence" of France? But we are learning—rapidly. When I was a student in London thirty years ago we regarded Japan as a fantastic joke; the comic opera, *The Mikado*, still preserves that foolish phase for the admiration of posterity. And to-day there is a quite unjustifiable tendency to ignore the quality of the Arab and of his religion. Islam is an open-air religion, noble and simple in its broad conceptions; it is none the less vital from Nigeria to China because it has sickened in the closeness of Constantinople. The French, the Italians, the British have to reckon with Islam and the Arab; where the continental deserts are, there the Arabs are and there is Islam; their culture will never be destroyed and replaced over these regions by Europeanism. The Allies who prepare the Peace of the World have to make their peace with that. And when I foreshadow this necessary liaison of the French and Arabic cultures, I am thinking not only of the Arab that is, but of the Arab that is to come. The whole trend of events in Asia Minor, the breaking up and decapitation of the Ottoman Empire and the Euphrates invasion, points to a great revival of Mesopotamia—at first under European direction. The vast system of irrigation that was destroyed by the Mongol armies of Hulugu in the thirteenth century will be restored; the desert will again become populous. But the local type will prevail. The new population of Mesopotamia will be neither European nor Indian; it will be Arabic; and with its concentration Arabic will lay hold of the printing press. A new intellectual movement in

Islam, a renascent Bagdad, is as inevitable as is 1950.

I have, however, gone a little beyond the discussion of the
future of the barbaric possessions in these anticipations of an
Arabic co-operation with the Latin peoples in the reconstruction of Western Asia and the barbaric regions of north and
central Africa. But regions of administered barbarism occur
not only in Africa. The point is that they are administered, and
that their economic development is very largely in the hands,
and will for many generations remain in the hands, of the
possessing country. Hitherto their administration has been in
the interests of the possessing nation alone. Their acquisition
has been a matter of bitter rivalries, their continued administration upon exclusive lines is bound to lead to dangerous
clashings. The common sense of the situation points to a
policy of give and take, in which throughout the possessions of
all the Pledged Allies, the citizens of all will have more or less
equal civil advantages. And this means some consolidation of
the general control of those Administered Territories. I have
already hinted at the possibility that the now exclusively British
navy may some day be a world-navy controlled by an
Admiralty representing a group of allies, Australasia, Canada,
Britain and, it may be, France and Russia and the United
States. To those who know how detached the British
Admiralty is at the present time from the general methods of
British political life, there will be nothing strange in this idea
of its completer detachment. Its personnel does to a large
extent constitute a class apart. It takes its boys out of the
general life very often before they have got to their fourteenth
birthday. It is not so closely linked up with specific British
social elements, with political parties and the general educational system, as are the rest of the national services.

There is nothing so very fantastic in this idea of a sort of
World-Admiralty; it is not even completely novel. Such bodies
as the Knights Templars transcended nationality in the Middle
Ages. I do not see how some such synthetic control of the seas
is to be avoided in the future. And now coming back to the
"White Man's Burthen," is there not a possibility that such a

board of marine and international control as the naval and international problems of the future may produce (or some closely parallel body with a stronger Latin element), would also be capable of dealing with these barbaric "Administered Territories"? A day may come when Tripoli, Nigeria, the French and the Belgian Congo will be all under one supreme control. We may be laying the foundations of such a system to-day unawares. The unstable and fluctuating conferences of the Allies to-day, their repeated experiences of the disadvantages of evanescent and discontinuous co-ordinations, may press them almost unconsciously toward this building up of things greater than they know.

We come now to the third and most difficult type of overseas "possessions." These are the annexed or conquered regions with settled populations already having a national tradition and culture of their own. They are, to put it bluntly, the suppressed, the overlaid, nations. Now I am a writer rather prejudiced against the idea of nationality; my habit of thought is cosmopolitan; I hate and despise a shrewish suspicion of foreigners and foreign ways; a man who can look me in the face, laugh with me, speak truth and deal fairly, is my brother though his skin is as black as ink or as yellow as an evening primrose. But I have to recognise the facts of the case. In spite of all my large liberality, I find it less irritating to be ruled by people of my own language and race and tradition, and I perceive that for the mass of people alien rule is intolerable.

Local difference, nationality, is a very obstinate thing. Every country tends to revert to its natural type. Nationality will out. Once a people has emerged above the barbaric stage to a national consciousness, that consciousness will endure. There is practically always going to be an Egypt, a Poland, an Armenia. There is no Indian nation, there never has been, but there are manifestly a Bengal and a Rajputana, there is manifestly a constellation of civilised nations in India. Several of these have literatures and traditions that extend back before the days when the Britons painted themselves with woad. Let us deal with this question mainly with reference to India.

What is said will apply equally to Burman or Egypt or Armenia or—to come back into Europe—Poland.

Now I have talked, I suppose, with many scores of people about the future of India, and I have never yet met anyone, Indian or British, who thought it desirable that the British should evacuate India at once. And I have never yet met anyone who did not think that ultimately the British must let the Indian nations control their own destinies. There are really not two opposite opinions about the destiny of India, but only differences of opinion as to the length of time in which that destiny is to be achieved. Many Indians think (and I agree with them) that India might be a confederation of sovereign states in close alliance with the British Empire and its allies within the space of fifty years or so. The opposite extreme was expressed by an old weary Indian administrator who told me, "Perhaps they may begin to be capable of self-government in four or five hundred years." These are the extreme Liberal and the extreme Tory positions in this question. It is a choice between decades and centuries. There is no denial of the inevitability of ultimate restoration. No one of any experience believes the British administration in India is an eternal institution.

There is a great deal of cant in this matter in Great Britain. Genteel English people with relations in the Indian Civil Service and habits of self-delusion, believe that Indians are "grateful" for British rule. The sort of "patriotic" self-flattery that prevailed in the Victorian age, and which is so closely akin to contemporary German follies, fostered and cultivated this sweet delusion. There are, no doubt, old ladies in Germany to-day who believe that Belgium will presently be "grateful" for the present German administration. Let us clear our minds of such cant. As a matter of fact no Indians really like British rule or think of it as anything better than a necessary, temporary evil. Let me put the parallel case to an Englishman or a Frenchman. Through various political ineptitudes our country has, we will suppose, fallen under the rule of the Chinese. They administer it, we will further assume, with an efficiency and honesty unparalleled in the bad old times of our lawyer politicians. They do not admit us to the higher branches of the administration; they go about our country wearing a strange costume, professing a strange religion—which implies that ours is wrong—speaking an unfamiliar tongue. They control our financial system and our economic development—on Chinese lines of the highest merit. They take the utmost care of our Gothic cathedrals for us. They put our dearest racial possessions into museums and admire them very much indeed. They teach our young men to fly kites and eat bird's nest soup. They do all that a well-bred people can do to conceal their habit and persuasion of a racial superiority. But they keep up their "prestige." ... You know, we shouldn't love them. It really isn't a question of whether they rule well or ill, but that the position is against certain fundamentals of human nature. The only possible footing upon which we could meet them with comfortable minds would be the footing that we and they were discussing the terms of the restoration of our country. Then indeed we might almost feel friendly with them. That is the case with all civilised "possessions." The only terms upon which educated British and Indians can meet to-day with any comfort is precisely that. The living intercourse of the British and Indian mind to-day is the discussion of the restoration. Everything else is humbug on the one side and self-deception on the other.

It is idle to speak of the British occupation of India as a conquest or a robbery. It is a fashion of much "advanced" literature in Europe to assume that the European rule of various Asiatic countries is the result of deliberate conquest with a view to spoliation. But that is only the ugly side of the facts. Cases of the deliberate invasion and spoliation of one country by another have been very rare in the history of the last three centuries. There has always been an excuse, and there has always been a percentage of truth in the excuse. The history of every country contains phases of political ineptitude in which that country becomes so misgoverned as to be not only a nuisance to the foreigner within its borders but a danger to its neighbours. Mexico is in such a phase to-day. And most of the aggressions and annexations of the modern period have arisen out of the inconveniences and reasonable fears caused by such an inept phase. I am a persistent advocate for the restoration of Poland, but at the same time it is very plain to me that it is a mere travesty of the facts to say that Poland, was a white lamb of a country torn to pieces by three wicked neighbours, Poland in the eighteenth century was a dangerous political muddle, uncertain of her monarchy, her policy, her affinities. She endangered her neighbours because there was no guarantee that she might not fall under the tutelage of one of them and become a weapon against the others.

The division of Poland was an outrage upon the Polish people, but it was largely dictated by an entirely honest desire to settle a dangerous possibility. It seemed less injurious than the possibility of a vacillating, independent Poland playing off one neighbour against another. That possibility will still be present in the minds of the diplomatists who will determine the settlement after the war. Until the Poles make up their minds, and either convince the Russians that they are on the side of Russia and Bohemia against Germany for evermore, or the Germans that they are willing to be Posenised, they will live between two distrustful enemies.

The Poles need to think of the future more and the wrongs of Poland less. They want less patriotic intrigue and more racial self-respect. They are not only Poles but members of a greater brotherhood. My impression is that Poland will "go Slav"—in spite of Cracow. But I am not sure. I am haunted by the fear that Poland may still find her future hampered by Poles who are, as people say, "too clever by half." An incalculable Poland cannot be and will not be tolerated by the rest of Europe.

And the overspreading of India by the British was in the same way very clearly done under compulsion, first lest the Dutch or French should exploit the vast resources of the peninsula against Britain, and then for fear of a Russian exploitation. I am no apologist for British rule in India; I think we have neglected vast opportunities there; it was our business from the outset to build up a free and friendly Indian confederation, and we have done not a tithe of what we might have done to that end. But then we have not done a little of what we might have done for our own country.

Nevertheless we have our case to plead, not only for going to India but—with the Berlin papers still babbling of Bagdad and beyond[3]—of sticking there very grimly. And so too the British have a fairly sound excuse for grabbing Egypt in their fear lest in its phase of political ineptitude it should be the means of strangling the British Empire as the Turk in Constantinople has been used to strangle the Russian. None of these justifications I admit are complete, but all deserve consideration. It is no good arguing about the finer ethics of the things that are; the business of sane men is to get things better. The business of all sane men in all the countries of the Pledged Allies and in America is manifestly to sink petty jealousies and a suicidal competitiveness, and to organise co-operation with all the intellectual forces they can find or develop in the subject countries, to convert these inept national systems into politically efficient independent organi-sations in a world peace alliance. If we fail to do that, then all the inept states and all the subject states about the world will become one great field for the sowing of tares by the enemy.

[Footnote 3: This was written late in February, 1916.]

So that with regard to the civilised just as with regard to the barbaric regions of the "possessions" of the European-centred empires, we come to the same conclusion. That on the whole the path of safety lies in the direction of pooling them and of declaring a common policy of progressive development leading to equality. The pattern of the United States, in which the procedure is first the annexation of "territories" and then their elevation to the rank of "States," must, with of course far more difficulty and complication, be the pattern for the "empires" of to-day—so far as they are regions of alien population. The path of the Dominions, settled by emigrants akin to the home population, Siberia, Canada, and so forth, to equal citizenship with the people of the Mother Country is by comparison simple and plain.

And so the discussion of the future of the overseas "empires" brings us again to the same realisation to which the discussion of nearly every great issue arising out of this war has pointed, the realisation of the imperative necessity of some great council or conference, some permanent overriding body, call it what you will, that will deal with things more broadly than any "nationalism" or "patriotic imperialism" can possibly do. That body must come into human affairs. Upon the courage and imagination of living statesmen it depends whether it will come simply and directly into concrete reality or whether it will materialise slowly through, it may be, centuries of blood and blundering from such phantom anticipations as this, anticipations that now haunt the thoughts of all politically-minded men.

XII

THE OUTLOOK FOR THE GERMANS

Section 1

Whatever some of us among the Allies may say, the future of
Germany lies with Germany. The utmost ambition of the
Allies falls far short of destroying or obliterating Germany; it is
to give the Germans so thorough and memorable an experience of war that they will want no more of it for a few
generations, and, failing the learning of that lesson, to make
sure that they will not be in a position to resume their military
aggressions upon mankind with any hope of success. After all,
it is not the will of the Allies that has determined even this
resolve. It is the declared and manifest will of Germany to
become predominant in the world that has created the Alliance
against Germany, and forged and tempered our implacable
resolution to bring militarist Germany down. And the nature
of the coming peace and of the politics that will follow the
peace are much more dependent upon German affairs than
upon anything else whatever.

This is so clearly understood in Great Britain that there is
scarcely a newspaper that does not devote two or three
columns daily to extracts from the German newspapers, and
from letters found upon German killed, wounded, or
prisoners, and to letters and descriptive articles from neutrals
upon the state of the German mind. There can be no doubt

H. G. Wells

that the British intelligence has grasped and kept its hold upon the real issue of this war with an unprecedented clarity. At the outset there came declarations from nearly every type of British opinion that this war was a war against the Hohenzollern militarist idea, against Prussianism, and not against Germany.

In that respect Britain has documented herself to the hilt. There have been, of course, a number of passionate outcries and wild accusations against Germans, as a race, during the course of the struggle; but to this day opinion is steadfast not only in Britain, but if I may judge from the papers I read and the talk I hear, throughout the whole English-speaking community, that this is a war not of races but ideas. I am so certain of this that I would say if Germany by some swift convulsion expelled her dynasty and turned herself into a republic, it would be impossible for the British Government to continue the war for long, whether it wanted to do so or not. The forces in favour of reconciliation would be too strong. There would be a complete revulsion from the present determination to continue the war to its bitter but conclusive end.

It is fairly evident that the present German Government understands this frame of mind quite clearly, and is extremely anxious to keep it from the knowledge of the German peoples. Every act or word from a British source that suggests an implacable enmity against the Germans as a people, every war-time caricature and insult, is brought to their knowledge. It is the manifest interest of the Hohenzollerns and Prussianism to make this struggle a race struggle and not merely a political struggle, and to keep a wider breach between the peoples than between the Governments. The "Made in Germany" grievance has been used to the utmost against Great Britain as an indication of race hostility. The everyday young German believes firmly that it was a blow aimed specially at Germany; that no such regulation affected any goods but German goods. And the English, with their characteristic heedlessness, have never troubled to disillusion him. But even the British caricaturist and the British soldier betray their fundamental opinion of the matter in their very insults. They will not use a word of abuse for the Germans as Germans; they call them "Huns," because they are thinking of Attila, because they are thinking of them as invaders under a monarch of peaceful France and Belgium, and not as a people living in a land of their own.

In Great Britain there is to this day so little hostility for Germans as such, that recently a nephew of Lord Haldane's, Sir George Makgill, has considered it advisable to manufacture race hostility and provide the Hohenzollerns with instances and quotations through the exertions of a preposterous Anti-German League. Disregarding the essential evils of the Prussian idea, this mischievous organisation has set itself to persuade the British people that the Germans are diabolical *as a race*. It has displayed great energy and ingenuity in pestering and insulting naturalised Germans and people of German origin in Britain—below the rank of the Royal Family, that is—and in making enduring bad blood between them and the authentic British. It busies itself in breaking up meetings at which sentiments friendly to Germany might be expressed, sentiments which, if they could be conveyed to German hearers, would certainly go far to weaken the determination of the German social democracy to fight to the end.

There can, of course, be no doubt of the good faith of Sir George Makgill, but he could do the Kaiser no better service than to help in consolidating every rank and class of German, by this organisation of foolish violence of speech and act, by this profession of an irrational and implacable hostility. His practical influence over here is trivial, thanks to the general good sense and the love of fair play in our people, but there can be little doubt that his intentions are about as injurious to the future peace of the world as any intentions could be, and there can be no doubt that intelligent use is made in Germany of the frothings and ravings of his followers. "Here, you see, is the disposition of the English," the imperialists will say to the German pacifists. "They are dangerous lunatics. Clearly we must stick together to the end." ...

H. G. Wells

The stuff of Sir George Makgill's league must not be taken as representative of any considerable section of British opinion, which is as a whole nearly as free from any sustained hatred of the Germans as it was at the beginning of the war. There are, of course, waves of indignation at such deliberate atrocities as the *Lusitania* outrage or the Zeppelin raids, Wittenberg will not easily be forgotten, but it would take many Sir George Makgills to divert British anger from the responsible German Government to the German masses.

That lack of any essential hatred does not mean that British opinion is not solidly for the continuation of this war against militarist imperialism to its complete and final defeat. But if that can be defeated to any extent in Germany by the Germans, if the way opens to a Germany as unmilitary and pacific as was Great Britain before this war, there remains from the British point of view nothing else to fight about. With the Germany of *Vorwaerts* which, I understand, would evacuate and compensate Belgium and Serbia, set up a buffer state in Alsace-Lorraine, and another in a restored Poland (including Posen), the spirit of the Allies has no profound quarrel at all, has never had any quarrel. We would only too gladly meet that Germany at a green table to-morrow, and set to work arranging the compensation of Belgium and Serbia, and tracing over the outlines of the natural map of mankind the new political map of Europe.

Still it must be admitted that not only in Great Britain but in all the allied countries one finds a certain active minority corresponding to Sir George Makgill's noisy following, who profess to believe that all Germans to the third and fourth generation (save and except the Hanoverian royal family domiciled in Great Britain) are a vile, treacherous, and impossible race, a race animated by an incredible racial vanity, a race which is indeed scarcely anything but a conspiracy against the rest of mankind.

The ravings of many of these people can only be paralleled by the stuff about the cunning of the Jesuits that once circulated in ultra-Protestant circles in England. Elderly Protestant ladies used to look under the bed and in the cupboard every night for a Jesuit, just as nowadays they look for a German spy, and as no doubt old German ladies now look for Sir Edward Grey. It may be useful therefore, at the present time, to point out that not only is the aggressive German idea not peculiar to Germany, not only are there endless utterances of French Chauvinists and British imperialists to be found entirely as vain, unreasonable and aggressive, but that German militarist imperialism is so little representative of the German quality, that scarcely one of its leading exponents is a genuine German.

Of course there is no denying that the Germans are a very distinctive people, as distinctive as the French. But their distinctions are not diabolical. Until the middle of the nineteenth century it was the fashion to regard them as a race of philosophical incompetents. Their reputation as a people of exceptionally military quality sprang up in the weed-bed of human delusions between 1866 and 1872; it will certainly not survive this war. Their reputation for organisation is another matter. They are an orderly, industrious, and painstaking people, they have a great respect for science, for formal education, and for authority. It is their respect for education which has chiefly betrayed them, and made them the instrument of Hohenzollern folly. Mr. F.M. Hueffer has shown this quite conclusively in his admirable but ill-named book, "When Blood is Their Argument." Their minds have been systematically corrupted by base historical teaching, and the inculcation of a rancid patriotism. They are a people under the sway of organised suggestion. This catastrophic war and its preparation have been their chief business for half a century; none the less their peculiar qualities have still been displayed during that period; they have still been able to lead the world in several branches of social organisation and in the methodical development of technical science. Systems of ideas are perhaps more readily shattered than built up; the aggressive patriotism of many Germans must be already darkened by serious doubts, and I see no inherent impossibility in hoping that the mass of the Germans may be restored to the common sanity of mankind, even in the twenty or thirty years of life that perhaps still remain for me.

Consider the names of the chief exponents of the aggressive German idea, and you will find that not one is German. The first begetter of Nietzsche's "blond beast," and of all that great flood of rubbish about a strange superior race with whitish hair and blue eyes, that has so fatally rotted the German imagination, was a Frenchman named Gobineau. We British are not altogether free from the disease. As a small boy I read the History of J.R. Green, and fed my pride upon the peculiar virtues of my Anglo-Saxon blood. ("Cp.," as they say in footnotes, Carlyle and Froude.) It was not a German but a renegade Englishman of the Englishman-hating Whig type, Mr. Houston Stewart Chamberlain, who carried the Gobineau theory to that delirious level which claims Dante and Leonardo as Germans, and again it was not a German but a British peer, still among us, Lord Redesdale, who in his eulogistic preface to the English translation of Chamberlain's torrent of folly, hinted not obscurely that the real father of Christ was not the Jew, Joseph, but a much more Germanic person. Neither Clausewitz, who first impressed upon the German mind the theory of ruthless warfare, nor Bernhardi, nor Treitschke, who did as much to build up the Emperor's political imagination, strike one as bearing particularly German names. There are indeed very grave grounds for the German complaint that Germany has been the victim of alien flattery and alien precedents. And what after all is the Prussian dream of world empire but an imitative response to the British empire and the adventure of Napoleon? The very title of the German emperor is the name of an Italian, Caesar, far gone in decay. And the backbone of the German system at the present time is the Prussian, who is not really a German at all but a Germanised Wend. Take away the imported and imposed elements from the things we fight to-day, leave nothing but what is purely and originally German, and you leave very little. We fight dynastic ambition, national vanity, greed, and the fruits of fifty years of basely conceived and efficiently conducted education.

The majority of sensible and influential Englishmen are fully aware of these facts. This does not alter their resolution to beat Germany thoroughly and finally, and, if Germany remains Hohenzollern after the war, to do their utmost to ring her in with commercial alliances, tariffs, navigation and exclusion laws that will keep her poor and powerless and out of mischief so long as her vice remains in her. But these considerations of the essential innocence of the German do make all this systematic hostility, which the British have had forced upon them, a very uncongenial and reluctant hostility. Pro-civilisation, and not Anti-German, is the purpose of the Allies. And the speculation of just how relentlessly and for how long this ring of suspicion and precaution need be maintained about Germany, of how soon the German may decide to become once more a good European, is one of extraordinary interest to every civilised man. In other words, what are the prospects of a fairly fundamental revolution in German life and thought and affairs in the years immediately before us?

H. G. Wells

Section 2

In a sense every European country must undergo revolutionary changes as a consequence of the enormous economic exhaustion and social dislocations of this war. But what I propose to discuss here is the possibility of a real political revolution, in the narrower sense of the word, in Germany, a revolution that will end the Hohenzollern system, the German dynastic system, altogether, that will democratize Prussia and put an end for ever to that secretive scheming of military aggressions which is the essential quarrel of Europe with Germany. It is the most momentous possibility of our times, because it opens the way to an alternative state of affairs that may supersede the armed watching and systematic war of tariffs, prohibitions, and exclusions against the Central Empires that must quite unavoidably be the future attitude of the Pledged Allies to any survival of the Hohenzollern empire.

We have to bear in mind that in this discussion we are dealing with something very new and quite untried hitherto by anything but success, that new Germany whose unification began with the spoliation of Denmark and was completed at Versailles. It is not a man's lifetime old. Under the state socialism and aggressive militarism of the Hohenzollern regime it had been led to a level of unexampled pride and prosperity, and it plunged shouting and singing into this war, confident of victories. It is still being fed with dwindling hopes of victory, no longer unstinted hopes, but still hopes—by a sort of political bread-card system. The hopes outlast the bread-and-butter, but they dwindle and dwindle. How is this parvenu people going to stand the cessation of hope, the realisation of the failure and fruitlessness of such efforts as no people on earth have ever made before? How are they going to behave when they realise fully that they have suffered and died and starved and wasted all their land in vain? When they learn too that the cause of the war was a trick, and the Russian invasion a lie? They have a large democratic Press that will not hesitate to tell them that, that does already to the best of its ability disillusion them. They are a carefully trained and educated and disciplined people, it is true[4]; but the solicitude of the German Government everywhere apparent, thus to keep the resentment of the people directed to the proper quarter, is, I think, just one of the things that are indicative of the revolutionary possibilities in Germany. The Allied Governments let opinion, both in their own countries and in America, shift for itself; they do not even trouble to mitigate the inevitable exasperation of the military censorship by an intelligent and tactful control. The German Government, on the other hand, has organised the putting of the blame upon other shoulders than its own elaborately and ably from the very beginning of the war. It must know its own people best, and I do not see why it should do this if there were not very dangerous possibilities ahead for itself in the national temperament.

[Footnote 4: A recent circular, which *Vorwaerts* quotes, sent by the education officials to the teachers of Frankfurt-am-Main, points out the necessity of the "beautiful task" of inculcating a deep love for the House of Hohenzollern (Crown Prince, grin and all), and concludes, "All efforts to excuse or minimise or explain the disgraceful acts which our enemies have committed against Germans all over the world are to be firmly opposed by you should you see any signs of these efforts entering the schools."]

It is one of the commonplaces of this question that in the past the Germans have always been loyal subjects and never made a revolution. It is alleged that there has never been a German republic. That is by no means conclusively true. The nucleus of Swiss freedom was the German-speaking cantons about the Lake of Lucerne; Tell was a German, and he was glorified by the German Schiller. No doubt the Protestant reformation was largely a business of dukes and princes, but the underlying spirit of that revolt also lay in the German national character. The Anabaptist insurrection was no mean thing in rebellions, and the history of the Dutch, who are, after all, only the extreme expression of the Low German type, is a history of the most stubborn struggle for freedom in Europe. This legend of German docility will not bear close examination. It is true that they are not given to spasmodic outbreaks, and that they do not lend themselves readily to intrigues and pronunciamentos, but there is every reason to suppose that they have the heads to plan and the wills to carry out as sound and orderly and effective a revolution as any people in Europe. Before the war drove them frantic, the German comic papers were by no means suggestive of an abject worship of authority and royalty for their own sakes. The teaching of all forms of morality and sentimentality in schools produces not only belief but reaction, and the livelier and more energetic the pupil the more likely he is to react rather than accept.

Whatever the feelings of the old women of Germany may be towards the Kaiser and his family, my impression of the opinion of Germans in general is that they believed firmly in empire, Kaiser and militarism wholly and solely because they thought these things meant security, success, triumph, more and more wealth, more and more Germany, and all that had come to them since 1871 carried on to the nth degree.... I do not think that all the schoolmasters of Germany, teaching in unison at the tops of their voices, will sustain that belief beyond the end of this war.

At present every discomfort and disappointment of the German people is being sedulously diverted into rage against the Allies, and particularly against the English. This is all very well as long as the war goes on with a certain effect of hopefulness. But what when presently the beam has so tilted against Germany that an unprofitable peace has become urgent and inevitable? How can the Hohenzollern suddenly abandon his pose of righteous indignation and make friends with the accursed enemy, and how can he make any peace at all with us while he still proclaims us accursed? Either the Emperor has to go to his people and say, "We promised you victory and it is defeat," or he has to say, "It is not defeat, but we are going to make peace with these Russian barbarians who invaded us, with the incompetent English who betrayed us, with all these degenerate and contemptible races you so righteously hate and despise, upon such terms that we shall never be able to attack them again. This noble and wonderful war is to end in this futility and—these graves. You were tricked into it, as you were tricked into war in 1870—but this time it has not turned out quite so well. And besides, after all, we find we can continue to get on with these people." ...

In either case, I do not see how he can keep the habitual and cultivated German hate pointing steadily away from himself. So long as the war is going on that may be done, but when the soldiers come home the hate will come home as well. In times of war peoples may hate abroad and with some unanimity. But after the war, with no war going on or any prospect of a fresh war, with every exploiter and every industrial tyrant who has made his unobtrusive profits while the country scowled and spat at England, stripped of the cover of that excitement, then it is inevitable that much of this noble hate of England will be seen for the cant it is. The cultivated hate of the war phase, reinforced by the fresh hate born of confusion and misery, will swing loose, as it were, seeking dispersedly for objects. The petty, incessant irritations of proximity will count for more; the national idea for less. The Hohenzollerns and the Junkers will have to be very nimble indeed if the German accomplishment of hate does not swing round upon them.

It is a common hypothesis with those who speculate on the probable effects of these disillusionments that Germany may break up again into its component parts. It is pointed out that Germany is, so to speak, a palimpsest, that the broad design of the great black eagle and the imperial crown are but newly painted over a great number of particularisms, and that these particularisms may return. The empire of the Germans may break up again. That I do not believe. The forces that unified Germany lie deeper than the Hohenzollern adventure; print, paper and the spoken word have bound Germany now into one people for all time. None the less those previous crowns and symbols that still show through the paint of the new design may help greatly, as that weakens under the coming stresses, to disillusion men about its necessity. There was, they will be reminded, a Germany before Prussia, before Austria for the matter of that. The empire has been little more than the first German experiment in unity. It is a new-fangled thing that came and may go again—leaving Germany still a nation, still with the sense of a common Fatherland.

Let us consider a little more particularly the nature of the mass of population whose collective action in the years immediately ahead of us we are now attempting to forecast. Its social strata are only very inexactly equivalent to those in the countries of the Pledged Allies. First there are the masses of the people. In England for purposes of edification we keep up the legend of the extreme efficiency of Germany, the high level of German education, and so forth. The truth is that the average *elementary* education of the common people in Britain is superior to that of Germany, that the domestic efficiency of the British common people is greater, their moral training better, and their personal quality higher. This is shown by a number of quite conclusive facts of which I will instance merely the higher German general death-rate, the higher German infantile death-rate, the altogether disproportionate percentage of crimes of violence in Germany, and the indisputable personal superiority of the British common soldier over his German antagonist. It is only when we get above the level of the masses that the position is reversed. The ratio of public expenditure upon secondary and higher education in Germany as compared with the expenditure upon elementary education is out of all proportion to the British ratio.

Directly we come to the commercial, directive, official, technical and professional classes in Germany, we come to classes far more highly trained, more alert intellectually, more capable of collective action, and more accessible to general ideas, than the less numerous and less important corresponding classes in Britain. This great German middle class is the strength and substance of the new Germany; it has increased proportionally to the classes above and below it, it has developed almost all its characteristics during the last half-century. At its lower fringe it comprehends the skilled and scientifically trained artisans, it supplies the brains of social democracy, and it reaches up to the world of finance and quasi-state enterprise. And it is the "dark horse" in all these speculations.

Hitherto this middle class has been growing almost unawares. It has been so busy coming into existence and growing, there has been so much to do since 1871, that it has had scarcely a moment to think round the general problem of politics at all. It has taken the new empire for granted as a child takes its home for granted, and its state of mind to-day must be rather like that of an intelligent boy who suddenly discovers that his father's picturesque and wonderful speculations have led to his arrest and brought the brokers into the house, and that there is nothing for it but to turn to and take control of the family affairs.

In Germany, the most antiquated and the most modern of European states, the old dynastic Germany of the princes and junkers has lasted on by virtue of exceptional successes and prestige into the world of steel and electricity. But their prestige has paled before the engineering of Krupp; their success evaporates. A new nation awakens to self-consciousness only to find itself betrayed into apparently irreconcilable hostility against the rest of mankind....

What will be the quality of the monarch and court and junkerdom that will face this awaking new Germany?

The monarch will be before very long the present Crown Prince. The Hohenzollerns have at least the merit of living quickly, and the present Emperor draws near his allotted term. He will break a record in his family if he lives another dozen years. So that quite soon after the war this new disillusioned Germany will be contemplating the imperial graces of the present Crown Prince. In every way he is an unattractive and uninspiring figure; he has identified himself completely with

H. G. Wells

that militarism that has brought about the European catastrophe; in repudiating him Germany will repudiate her essential offence against civilisation, and his appears to be the sort of personality that it is a pleasure to repudiate. He or some kindred regent will be the symbol of royalty in Germany through all those years of maximum stress and hardship ahead. Through-out the greater part of Germany the tradition of loyalty to his house is not a century old. And the real German loyalty is racial and national far more than dynastic. It is not the Hohenzollern over all that they sing about; it is Deutschland. (And—as in the case of all imperfectly civilised people—songs of hate for foreigners.) But it needed a decadent young American to sing:

"Thou Prince of Peace,
Thou God of War,"

to the dismal rhetorician of Potsdam. Real emperors reconcile and consolidate peoples, for an empire is not a nation; but the Hohenzollerns have never dared to be anything but sedulously national, "echt Deutsch" and advocates of black-letter. They know the people they have to deal with.

This new substantial middle mass of Germany has never been on friendly terms with the Germany of the court and the landowner. It has inherited a burgerlich tradition and resented even while it tolerated the swagger of the aristocratic officer. It tolerated it because that sort of thing was supposed to be necessary to the national success. But Munich, the comic papers, Herr Harden, *Vorwaerts*, speak, I think, for the central masses of German life far more truly than any official utterances do. They speak in a voice a little gross, very sensible, blunt, with a kind of heavy humour. That German voice one may not like, but one must needs respect it. It is, at any rate, not bombastic. It is essentially honest. When the imperial eagle comes home with half its feathers out like a crow that has met a bear; when the surviving aristocratic officers reappear with a vastly diminished swagger in the biergartens, I believe that the hitherto acquiescent middle classes and skilled artisan class of

German will entirely disappoint those people who expect them to behave either with servility or sentimental loyalty. The great revolutionary impulse of the French was passionate and generous. The revolutionary impulse of Germany may be even more deadly; it may be contemptuous. It may be they will not even drag emperor and nobles down; they will shove them aside....

In all these matters one must ask the reader to enlarge his perspectives at least as far back as the last three centuries. The galaxy of German monarchies that has over-spread so much of Europe is a growth of hardly more than two centuries. It is a phase in the long process of the break-up of the Roman Empire and of the catholic system that inherited its tradition. These royalties have formed a class apart, breeding only among themselves, and attempting to preserve a sort of caste internationalism in the face of an advance in human intelligence, a spread of printing, reading, and writing that makes inevitably for the recrudescence of national and race feeling, and the increasing participation of the people in government.

In Russia and England these originally German dynasties are meeting the problems of the new time by becoming national. They modify themselves from year to year. The time when Britain will again have a Queen of British race may not be very remote. The days when the affairs of Europe could be discussed at Windsor in German and from a German standpoint ended with the death of Queen Victoria, and it is only in such improvised courts as those of Greece and Bulgaria that the national outlook can still be contemplated from a foreign standpoint and discussed in a foreign tongue. The age when the monarchical system made the courts of three-quarters of Europe a German's Fatherland has ended for ever. And with that, the last rational advantage of monarchy and royalist sentimentality disappears from the middle-class German's point of view.

So it seems to me that the following conclusions about the future of Germany emerge from these considerations. It is improbable that there will be any such revolution as overthrew French Imperialism in 1871; the new Prussian Imperialism is closer to the tradition of the people and much more firmly established through the educational propaganda of the past half-century. But liberal forces in Germany may nevertheless be strong enough to force a peace upon the Hohenzollern empire so soon as any hopes of aggressive successes die away, before the utmost stage of exhaustion is reached, early in 1917, perhaps, or at latest in 1918. This, we suppose, will be a restrictive peace so far as Germany is concerned, humiliating her and hampering her development. The German Press will talk freely of a *revanche* and the renewal of the struggle, and this will help to consolidate the Pledged Allies in their resolve to hold Germany on every front and to retard her economic and financial recovery. The dynasty will lose prestige gradually, the true story of the war will creep slowly into the German consciousness, and the idea of a middle-class republic, like the French Republic, only defensively militant and essentially pacific and industrial, will become more and more popular in the country.

This will have the support of strong journalists, journalists of the Harden type for example. The dynasty tends to become degenerate, so that the probability of either some gross scandals or an ill-advised reactionary movement back to absolutism may develop a crisis within a few years of the peace settlement. The mercantile and professional classes will join hands with the social democrats to remove the decaying incubus of the Hohenzollern system, and Germany will become a more modern and larger repetition of the Third French republic. This collapse of the Germanic monarchical system may spread considerably beyond the limits of the German empire. It will probably be effected without much violence as a consequence of the convergence and maturity of many streams of very obvious thought. Many of the monarchs concerned may find themselves still left with their titles, palaces, and personal estates, and merely deprived of their last vestiges of legal power. The way will thus be opened for a gradual renewal of good feeling between the people of

Germany and the western Europeans. This renewal will be greatly facilitated by the inevitable fall in the German birthrate that the shortage and economies of this war will have done much to promote, and by the correlated discrediting of the expansionist idea. By 1960 or so the alteration of perspectives will have gone so far that historians will be a little perplexed to explain the causes of the Great War. The militarist monomania of Germany will have become incomprehensible; her *Welt Politik* literature incredible and unreadable....

Such is my reading of the German horoscope.

I doubt if there will be nearly so much writing and reading about the Great War in the latter half of the twentieth century as there was about Napoleon at the end of the nineteenth. The Great War is essentially undramatic, it has no hero, it has no great leaders. It is a story of the common sense of humanity suppressing certain tawdry and vulgar ideas and ambitions, and readjusting much that was wasteful and unjust in social and economic organisation. It is the story of how the spirit of man was awakened by a nightmare of a War Lord.... The nightmare will fade out of mind, and the spirit of man, with revivified energies, will set about the realities of life, the re-establishment of order, the increase of knowledge and creation. Amid these realities the great qualities of the Germans mark them for a distinguished and important role.

Section 3

The primary business of the Allies is not reconciliation with Germany. Their primary concern is to organise a great League of Peace about the world with which the American States and China may either unite or establish a permanent understanding. Separate attempts to restore friendship with the Germans will threaten the unanimity of the League of Peace, and perhaps renew the intrigues and evils of the Germanic dynastic system which this war may destroy. The essential restoration of Germany must be the work of German men speaking plain sense to Germans, and inducing their country to hold out its hand not to this or that suspicious neighbour but to mankind. A militarist Germany is a Germany self-condemned to isolation or world empire. A Germany which has returned to the ways of peace, on the other hand, will be a country that cannot be kept out of the system of civilisation. The tariff wall cannot but be lowered, the watchful restrictions cannot but be discontinued against such a Germany. Europe is a system with its heart half used, so long as Germany is isolated. The German population is and will remain the central and largest mass of people in Europe. That is a fact as necessary as the Indianism of India.

To reconstruct modern civilisation without Germany would be a colossal artificial task that would take centuries to do. It is inconceivable that Germany will stand out of Europeanism so long as to allow the trade routes of the world to be entirely deflected from her. Her own necessities march with the natural needs of the world.

So that I give the alliance for the isolation of Germany at the outside a life of forty years before it ceases to be necessary through the recovered willingness of the Germans to lay aside aggression.

But this is not a thing to be run at too hastily. It may be easily possible to delay this national general reconciliation of mankind by an unreal effusion. There will be no advantage in forcing the feelings of the late combatants. It is ridiculous to suppose that for the next decade or so, whatever happens, any Frenchmen are going to feel genial about the occupation of their north-east provinces, or any Belgians smile at the memory of Dinant or Louvain, or the Poles or Serbs forgive the desolation of their country, or any English or Russians take a humorous view of the treatment their people have had as prisoners in Germany. So long as these are living memories they will keep a barrier of dislike about Germany. Nor is it probable that the ordinary German is going to survey the revised map of Africa with a happy sense of relief, or blame no one but himself for the vanished prosperity of 1914. That is asking too much of humanity. Unless I know nothing of Germany, Germany will bristle with "denkmals" to keep open all such sores. The dislike of Germany by the allied nations will be returned in the hostility of a thwarted and disappointed people. Not even the neutrals will be aloof from these hostilities and resentments. The world will still, in 1950 or so, be throwing much passion into the rights and wrongs of the sinking of the *Lusitania*. There will be a bitterness in the memories of this and the next generation that will make the spectacle of ardent Frenchmen or Englishmen or Belgians or Russians embracing Germans with gusto—unpleasant, to say the least of it.

We may bring ourselves to understand, we may bring ourselves to a cold and reasonable forgiveness, we may suppress our Sir George Makgills and so forth, but it will take sixty or seventy years for the two sides in this present war to grow kindly again. Let us build no false hopes nor pretend to any false generosities. These hatreds can die out only in one way, by the passing of a generation, by the dying out of the wounded and the wronged. Our business, our unsentimental business, is to set about establishing such conditions that they will so die out. And that is the business of the sane Germans too. Behind the barriers this war will have set up between Germany and Anti-Germany, the intelligent men in either camp must prepare the ultimate peace they will never enjoy, must work for the days

H. G. Wells

when their sons at least may meet as they themselves can never meet, without accusation or resentment, upon the common business of the World Peace. That is not to be done by any conscientious sentimentalities, any slobbering denials of unforgettable injuries. We want no Pro-German Leagues any more than we want Anti-German Leagues. We want patience—and silence.

My reason insists upon the inevitableness and necessity of this ultimate reconciliation. I will do no more than I must to injure Germany further, and I will do all that I can to restore the unity of mankind. None the less is it true that for me for all the rest of my life the Germans I shall meet, the German things I shall see, will be smeared with the blood of my people and my friends that the wilfulness of Germany has spilt.

ABOUT THE AUTHOR

 **H. G. Wells** (September 21, 1866 – August 13, 1946), born Herbert George Wells, was an English writer best known for such science fiction novels as The Time Machine, The War of the Worlds, The Invisible Man, and The Island of Doctor Moreau. He was a prolific writer of both fiction and non-fiction, and produced works in many different genres, including contemporary novels, history, and social commentary. He was also an outspoken socialist. His later works become increasingly political and didactic, and only his early science fiction novels are widely read today. Wells, along with Hugo Gernsback and Jules Verne, is sometimes referred to as "The Father of Science Fiction".

Herbert George Wells, the fifth and last child of Joseph Wells (a former domestic gardener and at the time shopkeeper and cricketer) and his wife Sarah Neal (a former domestic servant), was born at Atlas House, 47 High Street, Bromley, Kent. The family was of the impoverished lower-middle-class.

A defining incident of young Wells's life is said to be an accident he had in 1874, when he was seven years old, which left him bedridden with a broken leg. To pass the time he started reading, and soon became devoted to the other worlds and lives to which books gave him access; they also stimulated his desire to write.

Choose from Thousands of 1stWorldLibrary Classics By

A. M. Barnard
Ada Leverson
Adolphus William Ward
Aesop
Agatha Christie
Alexander Aaronsohn
Alexander Kielland
Alexandre Dumas
Alfred Gatty
Alfred Ollivant
Alice Duer Miller
Alice Turner Curtis
Alice Dunbar
Allen Chapman
Alleyne Ireland
Ambrose Bierce
Amelia E. Barr
Amory H. Bradford
Andrew Lang
Andrew McFarland Davis
Andy Adams
Angela Brazil
Anna Alice Chapin
Anna Sewell
Annie Besant
Annie Hamilton Donnell
Annie Payson Call
Annie Roe Carr
Annonaymous
Anton Chekhov
Archibald Lee Fletcher
Arnold Bennett
Arthur C. Benson
Arthur Conan Doyle
Arthur M. Winfield
Arthur Ransome
Arthur Schnitzler
Arthur Train
Atticus
B.H. Baden-Powell
B. M. Bower
B. C. Chatterjee
Baroness Emmuska Orczy
Baroness Orczy
Basil King
Bayard Taylor
Ben Macomber
Bertha Muzzy Bower
Bjornstjerne Bjornson

Booth Tarkington
Boyd Cable
Bram Stoker
C. Collodi
C. E. Orr
C. M. Ingleby
Carolyn Wells
Catherine Parr Traill
Charles A. Eastman
Charles Amory Beach
Charles Dickens
Charles Dudley Warner
Charles Farrar Browne
Charles Ives
Charles Kingsley
Charles Klein
Charles Hanson Towne
Charles Lathrop Pack
Charles Romyn Dake
Charles Whibley
Charles Willing Beale
Charlotte M. Braeme
Charlotte M. Yonge
Charlotte Perkins Stetson
Clair W. Hayes
Clarence Day Jr.
Clarence E. Mulford
Clemence Housman
Confucius
Coningsby Dawson
Cornelis DeWitt Wilcox
Cyril Burleigh
D. H. Lawrence
Daniel Defoe
David Garnett
Dinah Craik
Don Carlos Janes
Donald Keyhoe
Dorothy Kilner
Dougan Clark
Douglas Fairbanks
E. Nesbit
E. P. Roe
E. Phillips Oppenheim
E. S. Brooks
Earl Barnes
Edgar Rice Burroughs
Edith Van Dyne
Edith Wharton

Edward Everett Hale
Edward J. O'Biren
Edward S. Ellis
Edwin L. Arnold
Eleanor Atkins
Eleanor Hallowell Abbott
Eliot Gregory
Elizabeth Gaskell
Elizabeth McCracken
Elizabeth Von Arnim
Ellem Key
Emerson Hough
Emilie F. Carlen
Emily Bronte
Emily Dickinson
Enid Bagnold
Enilor Macartney Lane
Erasmus W. Jones
Ernie Howard Pie
Ethel May Dell
Ethel Turner
Ethel Watts Mumford
Eugene Sue
Eugenie Foa
Eugene Wood
Eustace Hale Ball
Evelyn Everett-green
Everard Cotes
F. H. Cheley
F. J. Cross
F. Marion Crawford
Fannie E. Newberry
Federick Austin Ogg
Ferdinand Ossendowski
Fergus Hume
Florence A. Kilpatrick
Fremont B. Deering
Francis Bacon
Francis Darwin
Frances Hodgson Burnett
Frances Parkinson Keyes
Frank Gee Patchin
Frank Harris
Frank Jewett Mather
Frank L. Packard
Frank V. Webster
Frederic Stewart Isham
Frederick Trevor Hill
Frederick Winslow Taylor

Friedrich Kerst
Friedrich Nietzsche
Fyodor Dostoyevsky
G.A. Henty
G.K. Chesterton
Gabrielle E. Jackson
Garrett P. Serviss
Gaston Leroux
George A. Warren
George Ade
Geroge Bernard Shaw
George Cary Eggleston
George Durston
George Ebers
George Eliot
George Gissing
George MacDonald
George Meredith
George Orwell
George Sylvester Viereck
George Tucker
George W. Cable
George Wharton James
Gertrude Atherton
Gordon Casserly
Grace E. King
Grace Gallatin
Grace Greenwood
Grant Allen
Guillermo A. Sherwell
Gulielma Zollinger
Gustav Flaubert
H. A. Cody
H. B. Irving
H.C. Bailey
H. G. Wells
H. H. Munro
H. Irving Hancock
H. R. Naylor
H. Rider Haggard
H. W. C. Davis
Haldeman Julius
Hall Caine
Hamilton Wright Mabie
Hans Christian Andersen
Harold Avery
Harold McGrath
Harriet Beecher Stowe
Harry Castlemon
Harry Coghill
Harry Houidini

Hayden Carruth
Helent Hunt Jackson
Helen Nicolay
Hendrik Conscience
Hendy David Thoreau
Henri Barbusse
Henrik Ibsen
Henry Adams
Henry Ford
Henry Frost
Henry James
Henry Jones Ford
Henry Seton Merriman
Henry W Longfellow
Herbert A. Giles
Herbert Carter
Herbert N. Casson
Herman Hesse
Hildegard G. Frey
Homer
Honore De Balzac
Horace B. Day
Horace Walpole
Horatio Alger Jr.
Howard Pyle
Howard R. Garis
Hugh Lofting
Hugh Walpole
Humphry Ward
Ian Maclaren
Inez Haynes Gillmore
Irving Bacheller
Isabel Cecilia Williams
Isabel Hornibrook
Israel Abrahams
Ivan Turgenev
J.G.Austin
J. Henri Fabre
J. M. Barrie
J. M. Walsh
J. Macdonald Oxley
J. R. Miller
J. S. Fletcher
J. S. Knowles
J. Storer Clouston
J. W. Duffield
Jack London
Jacob Abbott
James Allen
James Andrews
James Baldwin

James Branch Cabell
James DeMille
James Joyce
James Lane Allen
James Lane Allen
James Oliver Curwood
James Oppenheim
James Otis
James R. Driscoll
Jane Abbott
Jane Austen
Jane L. Stewart
Janet Aldridge
Jens Peter Jacobsen
Jerome K. Jerome
Jessie Graham Flower
John Buchan
John Burroughs
John Cournos
John F. Kennedy
John Gay
John Glasworthy
John Habberton
John Joy Bell
John Kendrick Bangs
John Milton
John Philip Sousa
John Taintor Foote
Jonas Lauritz Idemil Lie
Jonathan Swift
Joseph A. Altsheler
Joseph Carey
Joseph Conrad
Joseph E. Badger Jr
Joseph Hergesheimer
Joseph Jacobs
Jules Vernes
Julian Hawthrone
Julie A Lippmann
Justin Huntly McCarthy
Kakuzo Okakura
Karle Wilson Baker
Kate Chopin
Kenneth Grahame
Kenneth McGaffey
Kate Langley Bosher
Kate Langley Bosher
Katherine Cecil Thurston
Katherine Stokes
L. A. Abbot
L. T. Meade

L. Frank Baum
Latta Griswold
Laura Dent Crane
Laura Lee Hope
Laurence Housman
Lawrence Beasley
Leo Tolstoy
Leonid Andreyev
Lewis Carroll
Lewis Sperry Chafer
Lilian Bell
Lloyd Osbourne
Louis Hughes
Louis Joseph Vance
Louis Tracy
Louisa May Alcott
Lucy Fitch Perkins
Lucy Maud Montgomery
Luther Benson
Lydia Miller Middleton
Lyndon Orr
M. Corvus
M. H. Adams
Margaret E. Sangster
Margret Howth
Margaret Vandercook
Margaret W. Hungerford
Margret Penrose
Maria Edgeworth
Maria Thompson Daviess
Mariano Azuela
Marion Polk Angellotti
Mark Overton
Mark Twain
Mary Austin
Mary Catherine Crowley
Mary Cole
Mary Hastings Bradley
Mary Roberts Rinehart
Mary Rowlandson
M. Wollstonecraft Shelley
Maud Lindsay
Max Beerbohm
Myra Kelly
Nathaniel Hawthrone
Nicolo Machiavelli
O. F. Walton
Oscar Wilde

Owen Johnson
P.G. Wodehouse
Paul and Mabel Thorne
Paul G. Tomlinson
Paul Severing
Percy Brebner
Percy Keese Fitzhugh
Peter B. Kyne
Plato
Quincy Allen
R. Derby Holmes
R. L. Stevenson
R. S. Ball
Rabindranath Tagore
Rahul Alvares
Ralph Bonehill
Ralph Henry Barbour
Ralph Victor
Ralph Waldo Emmerson
Rene Descartes
Ray Cummings
Rex Beach
Rex E. Beach
Richard Harding Davis
Richard Jefferies
Richard Le Gallienne
Robert Barr
Robert Frost
Robert Gordon Anderson
Robert L. Drake
Robert Lansing
Robert Lynd
Robert Michael Ballantyne
Robert W. Chambers
Rosa Nouchette Carey
Rudyard Kipling
Saint Augustine
Samuel B. Allison
Samuel Hopkins Adams
Sarah Bernhardt
Sarah C. Hallowell
Selma Lagerlof
Sherwood Anderson
Sigmund Freud
Standish O'Grady
Stanley Weyman
Stella Benson
Stella M. Francis

Stephen Crane
Stewart Edward White
Stijn Streuvels
Swami Abhedananda
Swami Parmananda
T. S. Ackland
T. S. Arthur
The Princess Der Ling
Thomas A. Janvier
Thomas A Kempis
Thomas Anderton
Thomas Bailey Aldrich
Thomas Bulfinch
Thomas De Quincey
Thomas Dixon
Thomas H. Huxley
Thomas Hardy
Thomas More
Thornton W. Burgess
U. S. Grant
Upton Sinclair
Valentine Williams
Various Authors
Vaughan Kester
Victor Appleton
Victor G. Durham
Victoria Cross
Virginia Woolf
Wadsworth Camp
Walter Camp
Walter Scott
Washington Irving
Wilbur Lawton
Wilkie Collins
Willa Cather
Willard F. Baker
William Dean Howells
William le Queux
W. Makepeace Thackeray
William W. Walter
William Shakespeare
Winston Churchill
Yei Theodora Ozaki
Yogi Ramacharaka
Young E. Allison
Zane Grey

www.ingramcontent.com/pod-product-compliance
Lightning Source LLC
Chambersburg PA
CBHW031343170626
46807CB00002B/807